AN IDEA OF
BOSNIA

ISBN 1-873796-58-7

Published by Autumn House
in association with Feed the Children

AN IDEA OF
BOSNIA

FEED THE CHILDREN

TAKING THE AID DIRECT

ACKNOWLEDGEMENTS

To The Spectator in which Raymond Tong's 'Not for Them' first appeared;

Robin Mellor's 'The Song of the Refugee Child' which was first published in Assemblies, (Scholastic Books, 1994);

Louise Hudson's 'Globe Light', first published in Slow Dancer Magazine and also in Intimate Relations, (Stride Publications);

To Second Shift No 4, 1994 for Anne Born's poem 'Going On';

Gerald England's 'Square 7e', published in Printed Matter (Japan) and International Journal on World Peace (USA);

Judith Kazantzis's 'To the Island', published in Bete Noire;

Katherine Gallagher's 'The Long Reach Out of War' from Passengers to the City, (Hale and Iremonger 1985);

'Emina' by Aleksa Šantić, Fourteenth century Mostar poet (Serb), as part of Reminiscences;

'Jape' by Sonja Besford, translated (from Serbian) by Christina Pribičević-Zorić and from How to Catch the Thallason, Prosveta, Belgrade, 1992;

Opening of 'Propaganda' — quote from broadcast by Croatia Radio, Mostar, April 1993;

'The War Process' by Benjamin Zephaniah, © Benjamin Zephaniah 1994;

'Crossing the Border' by Carole Satyamurti appears in her book Striking Distance, (OUP 1994);

To Critical Quarterly, volume 35, number 3, 1993 for Tony Lopez's 'No one Takes a Profit' also collected in Stress Management and other poems, published by Boldface Press, 1994;

To Smoke and Dusting Round the Jelly (Odyssey Publications) for Mary Maher's 'Dividing the World';

To The New Statesman and Society for Alison Fell's 'The Truce';

To Seam in which Michael Laskey's 'The Burn' first appeared;

Adèle Geras's 'In the Queue for Water' from her book Voices from the Dolls' House, published by The Rockingham Press;

Harry Guest's 'Our History was like a Deserted Street' which first appeared in The Wide Skirt To the New Statesman and Society for David Grubb's 'An Idea of Bosnia';

Duncan Bush's 'Living in Real Times', © Duncan Bush, first published in Masks by Duncan Bush (Severn Books 1994);

Yvonne Burns's translation of 'Evening on the Island' by Aleksa Šantić published in An Encyclopaedia of World Poetry;

Igor Klikovac's 'September, Beginning of Winter' translated by Vanja Karas and Richard Beresford from the Bosnian;

To Staple Magazine for 'The Diplomats at Christmas' by David Goodall which appeared in their winter issue of 1994;

To Stand Magazine for 'The Trials of the Man of Ca' by W. M. Reynolds;

Yann Lovelock's 'Abandoning the Mountain' has appeared in Poesie Europe (Frankfurt, 1995) and his collection Landscape with Voices (University of Salzburg Press, 1995);

Anthony Rollinson's 'Remember Me' was first published in Mixed-Up (Responses Publications, 1994);

Philip Gross's 'How It Happens' to appear in Scratch City (Faber);

Peter Dale's 'Utterance' first appeared in The Swansea Review;

Mario Petrucci's 'Smoking in Sarajevo' was a prize winner in the 1995 Peace and Freedom Competition, and appeared in the winners' anthology;

Rupert Loydell's 'Thoughts of Resistance' was first published in Between Dark Dreams by Acumen Publications;

Phil Carradice's 'Pictures of Bosnia' was first broadcast in BBC Radio Wales;

Anne Beresford's 'Reading Lesson' first appeared in her book of poems Landscape with Figures, published by Agenda Editions, 1994;

Mike Jenkins's 'Vedran Smailovic' was first published in This House, My Ghetto by Seren Books, 1995;

Tony Curtis's 'The Front' is from his book War Voices published by Seren Books.

IMPORTANT NOTICE. DECLARATION: Every attempt has been made to keep each contributor fully informed about our use of their materials. Acknowledging every item has not been possible due to extreme difficulties in a world where contact addresses change rapidly. We apologize to anybody whom we have not been able to communicate with, before this book went to press.
George Solly, Feed the Children, November 1995

FOREWORD

Earlier this year I asked to be allowed to visit Bosnia to see the work of Feed the Children at first hand.

From the moment I arrived at their warehouse in Split, and more so as we drove into central Bosnia and I met the distribution teams, I saw that aid distribution is no different from any business. It can operate well or badly. My job was to watch, listen and learn.

I watched the villagers' faces as we delivered baby food and supplies to the remotest places. I listened to the needs of a particular refugee family living in one small room as they spoke with dignity and courage. And I thought of my own family.

I listened as the doctor and nurses at Travnik Hospital conferred with the team about aid received in the past and help needed in the future.

I learned of Feed the Children's project to supply each child daily with a bread roll at school, thereby ensuring a measure of nourishment and regular education. I learned that in war society breaks down, leaving people without the simple, basic, everyday needs.

And I saw that Feed the Children is there, supplying many of those needs. During their three years in Bosnia, Feed the Children has painstakingly built up a web of contacts, a reputation and a trust that will allow them to continue to reach those in greatest need. It was this reputation and ground work that enabled their aid deliveries into the cut-off enclave of Bihac to get through when others could not. There they found 10,000 babies and children in great need. Some had already died, many were born prematurely due to their mothers' psychological trauma and malnourishment. More died due to lack of nutritional food. And older children, injured by the shelling, died because there was insufficient food to help them recover.

There are many more areas in such great need, with thousands more children who need our help to get them through this madness.

Like you, perhaps, I've often wondered how much of the pound we give reaches its destination. My time in Bosnia showed me that Feed the Children is nothing if not an efficient business, run with flair, courage and determination by extraordinary people. They are fast becoming one of the most respected Aid Agencies working in Bosnia.

If, like me, you want to help the children, I believe there can be no better way than by supporting Feed the Children. Whatever you can afford, I've now seen for myself, will be well used and immensely appreciated.

AN IDEA OF
BOSNIA

CONTENTS

AN IDEA IN IMAGES 10

Nigel Dickinson and the FTC Photo Library

AN IDEA IN PROSE 42

AN IDEA IN POETRY 161

AN IDEA FROM FIELD REPORTS 201

PEOPLE TO PEOPLE 266

BUILDING THE PEACE 276

AN IDEA OF
BOSNIA

CONCEPT

Feed the Children is an aid agency responding to the needs of children, mothers and carers in extreme need created by man-made or natural disasters. Since 1990 we have taken aid to Romania, Bulgaria, the Kurdish refugees, to Albania, Croatia and Bosnia, to Rwanda, Haiti and the Caucasus. This adds up to £31m worth of aid, comprising food, medicines, blankets, clothing and educational material.

Following the success of *Klaonica*, a poetry anthology published by Bloodaxe for FTC, we have created a new book, *An Idea of Bosnia*.

This contains photographs, artwork, poems and prose, as well as field reports designed to enhance awareness of the problems, the pain, but also of the possibilities. Whenever peace comes, and in whatever form, the need will change but not go away for many years and this book will assist in FTC continuing its vital role.

CONTRIBUTORS

Contributors include: Martin Booth — Alan Bold — Judith Kazantzis — Helen Dunmore — Peter Dent — Tony Curtis — Paul Groves — Raymond Tong — Mario Petrucci — Phillip Gross — Carole Satyamurti — Harry Guest — Tony Lopez — John Mole — Duncan Forbes — Peter Dale — Yann Lovelock — Alison Fell — Jenny Joseph — Oliver Burch — Mišo Maric — Nerma Dizdarevic — Sonja Besford — W. M. Reynolds

GRAPHICS
C. Radley

PHOTOGRAPHS
Nigel Dickinson / Leader Photos and the FTC Library

Nigel Dickinson is a freelance photojournalist whose experience ranges from reportage of Squatter Groups in South Africa in the early eighties; a book on the Miners Strike (Spokesman Press, 'Hanging on by Your Fingernails'); documentation of Land Rights and Deforestation in South-east Asia, which won him a UNEP award at the 1992 Earth Summit in Rio; to his exhibitions 'Road' in 1994 and 'People and the Land' in 1995, commissioned by Staffordshire County Council. Nigel also has worked on photographing Gypsies / Gitan in France and Spain. He has been widely published in magazines across Europe and the USA.

AN IDEA OF
BOSNIA

The publication of *Klaonica, Poems for Bosnia* (Bloodaxe 1993), did many things. It raised funds for aid work undertaken by Feed the Children, it raised awareness at readings and in the literary magazines, it also gave poets the opportunity to express ideas that went beyond the immediate conflict, the barbarity, the politics. There are war photographers, war reporters, war artists and the best of these reach beyond the killing; so why not poets? Or is war poetry to be neatly proscribed to warn of the past, written in reflection, reactive? Or is it that the artist has to write from personal experience when dealing with war, unlike most other subjects? The 'debate' that was raised was peculiarly British, stemming from the concept that poetry can only be passive, can never make things happen, a protest of passion but never a practicality. American poets writing about Vietnam evidently never believed this. Irish poets writing about 'the troubles' didn't accept this. Poets in China and Romania, Russia and Albania took risks with words. And the question is still asked about those writers in Germany who didn't use words as weapons to declare the greatest inhumanity of this century. So, why not write out our ideas about former Yugoslavia? Why not seek beyond the media metaphors, the shooting, the sound bite trite, the edited view?

The words and images, the ideas, the forward impulse of this book seek to go beyond what has already been reported on screens and on the page and in interview-speak. These are the impressions and definitions of poets and children, of photographers, aid workers and citizens, a merging of minds and meanings.

This book will raise more funds, more awareness, more insights about the particular nature of a civil war, terrorism, horror politics, where the leaders have no territory but war and the civilians are specific targets.

No matter how long it takes, an idea of Bosnia will one day blossom into a positive reality. The ogres will go. The babies and children that we have saved will turn a territory of 'no' into a country of 'yes'. Like all good ideas, this idea of Bosnia needs to be heard and watched and made welcome.

All contributors to this book have given freely and speedily and enthusiastically. This is, therefore, an anthology of possibility, a challenge to reality, a refusal simply to accept the facts as knowledge. Knowledge is response to the terror, taking us beyond.

DAVID H. W. GRUBB
Executive Director, Feed the Children

AN IDEA IN
IMAGES

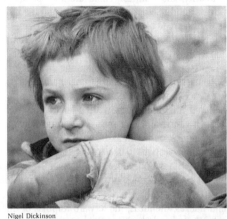

Nigel Dickinson

Refugee hostel, Travnik, Bosnia

Travnik, Bosnia

Nigel Dickinson

Violent playgrounds, Bosnia

Gornji Vakuf, Bosnia

◀ Gornji Vakuf, Bosnia

Gornji Vakuf, Bosnia

Nigel Dickinson

Nigel Dickinson

Refugee hostel, Travnik, Bosnia

Nigel Dickinson

Gornji Vakuf, Bosnia

Another winter, Bosnia

Travnik, Bosnia ▶

Travnik, Bosnia

◄ Refugee hostel, Travnik, Bosnia

Metkovic,
Croatia
Nigel Dickinson

Nigel Dickinson

The good earth, Bosnia

Nigel Dickinson

The soil that saves, Bosnia

The ravaged land, Bosnia
Nigel Dickinson

Refugees near Split, Croatia

Nigel Dickinson

Maglaj, Bosnia

Cemetery scene ▶
Travnik, Bosnia

Nigel Dickinson

Fallen faiths, Bosnia

Mostar, Bosnia

Nigel Dickinson

Nigel Dickinson

Mostar, Bosnia

Barrel Bomb Alley, Gornji Vakuf, Bosnia   Nigel Dickinson

Nigel Dickinson

FTC aid convoy, Bosnia

AN IDEA IN
PROSE

JAPE

by Sonja Besford

Translated (from Serbian) by Christina Pribičević-Zorić

I never know whether I am dreaming, whether I am imagining it or whether that scene on the narrow road is, in some unknown dimension, real. The road is lined with tall birch trees, and behind them is a field of lush willows. They seem to sprout from the water, parading their insouciance. The sun is scorching hot, the road quivers in the air. Not a living soul is in sight. I am standing there in a strange outfit: a long coat, a high-collared white shirt, a tie that is choking me. I am waiting for her. I always wait for her in exactly the same place. She appears at the end of the road, first as a black spot, then as a tiny figure who becomes larger and larger, until soon I recognize her blue silk dress, waist-long hair and pale face that looks as though it had never been caressed by the sun. I stand stock still, hardly daring to breathe. My heart is gripped by the anticipation of revelation. I know I must not move because if I do she will disappear, this woman I keep waiting for. She approaches me with a smile and open arms. I draw her into my embrace, drinking in the scent of camomile and sun in her hair. We stand like that for a long time, not uttering a word, except that I think: let this moment wait for its end, let it be patient. Then I tell her voicelessly about things living and dead. About sorrows and joys. About memories and events. I tell her, and she kisses my eyes and my lips. Then she tells me, and I kiss her. I believe her. I love her. I want her.

I am woken in the morning by the smell of coffee. My body and heart are still on that narrow road, on her flesh, but the duties of reality propel me out of bed. I can hear the family. There is always a door slamming somewhere. And the phone has started ringing.

Later, in the office, Milan immediately knows that I went travelling last night. He says he can always see a strange tenderness, a mysterious remoteness, in my eyes. He also says my love is real, the Fates were generous, we do live in a secret world, in a divine foam that only dreamers suspect. I once told him that I would give almost anything to find her now, in this life. Milan says: 'Dream and be grateful. The Fates do not open the secret doors to just anyone.'

All the same, I would give it all up, I would forsake everything for her.

Dragitsa is rushing around the house. She is straightening the pictures, dusting the place for the third time, grumbling that I forgot to buy beer. I watch her: she is still good-looking. Especially today with make-up on, slender. We are expecting our son, he is bringing his fiancé and her parents. Until the other day I didn't even know that Srdjan was in love, that he had serious intentions.

'Sit down, Dragitsa, please. You're making me dizzy, calm down. Let's have a drink before the guests arrive,' I say, although I don't feel like a drink. I feel ten centuries old, worn out by life. I feel that I've been worshipping lies.

'Oh, it's easy for you! You won't be blamed if the house isn't in order,' replies Dragitsa, but she sits down all the same. I pour us some wine. Dragitsa lights a cigarette, gazing off into space.

'It's gone by so fast . . . '

'What has?' I ask, knowing what she means.

'Time . . . the years . . . . It seems like only yesterday that we were rocking Srdjan in his cradle. Remember? Thirty years ago . . . I can't believe it, although . . . all in all, we can't complain. We've done all right . . . . What do you think?' she asks, and I avert my eyes. What can I tell her? I don't hesitate. I have got to continue the way I started — with lies.

'Yes, we have. You've met her. . . . What's she like?'

'Yasmina?'

'Mmmm . . . '

'She's pretty, she's bright. . . . They get along well. . . . She says she can't cook and I told her that was smart of her. Why reek of onions and fried oil all the time? Anyway, everything's changing now, even a woman's wretched role in the kitchen. I suppose it'll be all right. . . .'

I nod my head, I see she is trying not to be a future mother-in-law. She loves Srdjan, and she will love Yasmina, as long as he does. Later, who knows?

I hear Srdjan unlocking the door. Voices. Dragitsa stands up, smiling from ear to ear. She goes to greet her guests. I walk over to the window. It has started to rain. It's a real summer shower. I open the window to inhale the smouldering smells. The mown grass, the roses, the gloomy touches of long-since extinguished loves. In the street children are playing 'caught in the fire'. The rain doesn't bother them, they are enjoying the vanity of the sudden downpour, they have their youthful naïvety firmly in hand. I really do envy them: my own fires burned out long ago, and, in between, decked out in lies, I count the days, like an impatient nestling. Did I ever really love Dragitsa? Did I ever belong to love, home or self? Am I present? Do I know Dragitsa? Srdjan? Myself? No. No.

'Dad, this is Yasmina. Yasmina this is my father,' I hear Srdjan say.

I set my lips into a softly welcoming smile. I love Srdjan, I shall love Yasmina. I turn around. Gazing at me is a young woman with waist-length hair and a pale face that looks as though it had never been caressed by the sun. My smile freezes. My heart leaps. I cannot move or utter a word. I feel the blood rush to my head, everything seems blurred and unsteady. I see that she is walking over to me, her hand held out. I take it.

'Haven't we met before?' I hear her say, as though from a distance. I want to collect myself, to return, to exist. I am still holding her hand, trying to escape her inquisitive eyes.

'Could be, the world is getting smaller and smaller,' I mumble, surprised by the banality of my own words.

She will never be mine. She has run down the narrow road to meet Srdjan. She has stepped out of the dream, the invisible world, the foam of the dreamer. Now at least I know that her name *was* Yasmina. I feel sick. Srdjan is looking at me, waiting for me to become a father. Now at least I know that her name *is* Yasmina. I kiss her on the cheek, mumbling a few words of welcome. Her hair smells of camomile.

* * *

We are sitting at the dinner table. We have had quite a lot of wine. The conversation is cheerful and I stopped stammering hours ago. Yasmina's father is a scowling but witty man, her mother is pretty — and secretive like a cul-de-sac. Yasmina keeps turning that unerringly distant look on me: she is trying to remember where we met before. Srdjan is in love. Dragitsa is charming. I repose in the peace of a man who knows that he will be executed in the morning and that the pitiless, spiteful Fates will not allow a pardon.

I get up to carry the plates out into the kitchen. There I am safe. I lean my brow against the cold refrigerator door. The death of a dream is worse than the death of life. Is there a cemetery of dreams somewhere? What would I plant on my dream-grave? My severed head or my anger? Sacred herbs or nettles?

'I remember now . . . ,' I heard her say. I turn around, take a step forward and stand in front of Yasmina.

'It was a long time ago. I dreamt of a narrow road and you were coming towards . . . .'

I stroke her burning cheek to stop the words that I do not wish to hear today. Not today. Not yet. Her eyes wet, Yasmina kisses the palm of my hand. I tremble in the now clear realization that as of tomorrow, Yasmina and I shall repeat what was and, grateful to the Fates, love whatever will be. Secretly.

PROPAGANDA

'Dear people of Mostar, we are sorry to tell you that this morning, in our beautiful city, a Muslim sniper, a man with moustaches known as Osman, interrupted the beating of the hearts of three of our dearest citizens: Hasanović Ragib, Kapić Miro and Mladnović Sretan, who were peacefully walking in Fejić Street. So doped with narcotics was this Muslim sniper, this vile assassin, that he was shooting at his own people on the left side of the river.' (Broadcast by Croatian Radio, Mostar, April 1993.)

I don't know why I think about Mustafa and Amra more often than others who were good friends in Mostar. Perhaps I could say that they were my best friends. I remember very well when Amra had a little baby girl which they named Aida. She was so tiny and pink, like a little peach, the smallest child I have ever seen. Amra was so proud of this little mite, and of her husband too. We celebrated their daughter together, with all our friends. Later she had a second child, another little girl, named Jasmina or Mina.

The Delić family were not intellectuals in the ordinary sense. You wouldn't hear talk of literature or history or politics in their home. But as soon as you entered there was a coffee in front of you; then lemonade, home-made brandy and *meze*. There would be Bosnian folk music playing on the tape recorder and you could relax completely. There was nothing to worry about, nothing to be upset about. All the children were in a separate room playing together. You could use the house as if it were your own. The main interests for adults were the brandy and the music.

Mustafa was a journalist, but rarely worked as one under the Communist system. For most of the time I knew him, he was a supervisor in one of the local factories. He was actually a very intelligent man but, under the previous system, intelligence was not always regarded as a positive thing. Mustafa probably decided to be like everybody else because it was the easy way to go. I used to blame him for that, but not any more. Mustafa spent most of his spare time fly-fishing in the Neretva.

At the beginning Mustafa and Amra believed in the future of Bosnia-Hercegovina for all its people. Later they believed in the Mostar Brigade, and felt very secure and protected with the Bosnian army in town. They were not worried for their own safety, confident that Mostar could be under Muslim control within twenty-four hours. Mustafa had enlisted in the Brigade. He was fishing as often as before. Fresh trout fetched a good price in a city living on aid. Whenever I drank a coffee with them I couldn't help but give my opinion, which was not optimistic. When I told them I was going to Germany, they couldn't understand me at all.

'The Croats can hate us but nothing more,' they would tell me.

And then in April the war between so-called friends began for the first time in Mostar: heavy shooting with anti-aircraft artillery between the two sides all night long and snipers in the morning, followed by the strange silence of empty streets. Later in the afternoon I was sitting in front of our block of flats with our neighbours when Mustafa and his father-in-law came running, very upset and frightened.

'There's a sniper by the surgery,' Mustafa said. 'He killed the man queuing in front of me.'

We invited them up to the apartment to give them water and sugar, and then they had to go.

It was a false start. Muslims and Croats didn't begin the real war that time, and everything was quiet after a couple of days, though still tense. I started work again, and got my passport. I wanted to go to Germany, and desperately asked questions about the arrangements. One day I was told that somebody was at the door to see me and I went to the waiting room. There was Amra, very excited and very frightened.

'Please, can you put me on the list for Germany?' she begged.

I took her to see my boss, and he put her on the list. Then I gave her some coffee and we had a chat. She seemed more relaxed and not quite so terrified.

'Don't worry, we'll go together,' I told her.

Two or three days before the war between Muslims and Croats really began, I visited Mustafa and Amra again. They were completely different people. All the confidence was gone.

'HVO and the Croats are very strong,' Mustafa kept saying. That was the last time I saw either of my dear friends. We never made it to Germany, though later I escaped without them.

NERMA DIZDAREVIĆ, AUGUST 1993

Dear Nerma,

I am OK and doing well. I am waiting to go to Italy, but at the moment not even a bird can leave this city. At the first opportunity I shall leave. All the papers are ready. It is awful here. There are a lot of people on the left side now. All the people who were originally there, and the others sent from the right side to the left. Every day, ten to twenty civilians are killed on the left side. There are just a few Muslims left on the right side and they are having the hardest time. They are afraid of everybody and they don't have enough food. Those with a little money are still all right. There are only soldiers on the streets, and they are shooting, they are drunk, they are horrible.

Nobody knows if their family is safe. It's better not to ask too many questions. It's tense and full of hatred. There is nothing left here. From Hit to Liska Street, the Boulevard and Santić Street, everything has been flattened. Absolutely destroyed and burned. Huge amounts of ruins and a lot of smoke. It stinks of rubbish and of the dead bodies which have sometimes been lying on the street for two or three days. It's still very hot which makes everything worse. I never expected anything like this. Horrible. Absolutely everybody is shelling, *ćetniks* to the left side lately. Everybody is mad here. Nobody is normal any more. A city of mad people — and the dead. That is Mostar.

They killed Mustafa and Aida on the street. Amra and Mina are on the left side. The radio says they killed all the Hadjimusic family in the flat. Impossible things are happening here. I won't tell you all the news of people who have been killed, because there is no point in upsetting you more. Your mother is sewing Croat flags for the HVO (The Bosnian Croat Army). That will help her for a while, prevent her being sent to the left side. Dragana helped her a lot. You should be grateful to her that your mother is still alive. Maybe it would be better for her if she were not. But your mother doesn't panic, and she says she wants to survive and see all her children again.

We get food from our friends, not much, but we are not hungry. My Croatian friends saved my life. You know who they are, and they all send their regards to you. It isn't safe to say more. I don't know how long I am staying here, but as soon as I can get out I'll call you. If I am lucky it will be soon.

Nobody will ever live comfortably in this city again. People hate each other too much. There is no trust. A Muslim will never trust a Croat again, and the other way round. The Old Bridge is shaking and it will fall down in a matter of days. There is a lot of propaganda from both sides on the radio. Our politicians should have avoided this. This shouldn't have happened. Love to everybody,

ZLATKO, MOSTAR, 25 SEPTEMBER 1993.

Almost as soon as I got into Mostar after the ceasefire I went to see the Delić family. Nerma had given me the address of Amra's father and mother on the left side, in the little suburb of Donja Mahala. I had never met Amra or Mina, but Nerma was sure they would be living with her parents. In England I had watched Nerma pack a little rucksack full of chocolate and coffee and other good things for them, tucking her letter inside the flap.

'Can we give Amra just a few German marks?' she had asked me. I knew that Amra had been her best friend.

I had known my way all over Mostar at the beginning of the war with the Serbs, but now I hardly recognized the left side. It was a place of ruined walls and piles of rubble, stark chimney stacks standing above collapsed roofs and people living in cellars. There had been no electricity or water on this side of the city for nearly two years. As you entered every building the smell from the toilet hit you before anything else. Little cemeteries had appeared wherever there was a convenient place to dig, usually in parks or children's playgrounds. Each mound of fresh, reddish earth was capped with a wooden headboard painted with a green crescent, a name, and always the same date: 1993. There would be fresh wild flowers and sometimes the sad purple shield and golden lilies of Bosnia.

The old Turkish suburb of Donja Mahala lies across the river, close beneath the grey flank of Mount Hum. As I waited for my knock to be answered, I could see the red and white Croatian flag flickering above their militia's forward positions on the summit. Mrs Delić asked me in to wait; Amra was on Hum collecting firewood for the stove, as she did every day, but she would not be long. I knew that Amra was qualified as a lawyer, but talk of such achievements only made Mostar people smile now. Those things belonged to another world. Everybody needed firewood. Someone handy with a sharp axe was of more use than any lawyer.

Amra came in with her bundle of logs while I was talking to little Mina by the stove. She was just as Nerma had described her to me: slim and graceful, with wide green eyes and a sad smile. There were tears when she read Nerma's letter while little Mina beamed at the sight of the bars of chocolate. I had to tell her how very sad we have been to hear about Mustafa and Aida.

Suddenly the tears somehow became mixed with laughter and smiles all at once.

'Oh, no . . . it's not true,' Amra was saying, to my complete amazement. 'Radio . . . lies . . . just lies.'

I took some convincing. But Amra led me at once to the little Donja Mahala school, which never closed for a day during the siege, and little embarrassed Aida was hauled out from her class in a basement to meet me and have her photograph taken for Nerma. Then Amra took me across the river on one of the

51

improvised wire bridges where sniper curtains flapped in the wind, and then down into a deep cellar full of tobacco smoke and packed with men in battledress working at desks. One of them rose at once to his feet. Amra explained the situation. We flung our arms around each other like old friends. This was Mustafa, working now for Bosnian Army Intelligence. The whole family had made it safely to the left side.

We had a party that night in Donja Mahala with a bottle of *rakia* which Mustafa produced somehow. It was like drinking with Lazarus; to me there was still something miraculous about that man. We couldn't speak each other's language, but it didn't seem to matter. We found that we were both trout fishermen, so we drew each other diagrams of flies and casts, and boasted about weights in kilograms and pounds. It's all fixed now; we're going to fish the Neretva together after the war.

Two hours after curfew Mustafa insisted on seeing me back to the cellar I was sleeping in across the river. We were both slightly drunk and very happy, but the cold air outside sobered us up with a shock. A clammy mist had risen up from the river. The night soldiers had gone up to the front line along the Boulevard hours before; after the usual outbreak of shots (here there is almost no such thing as a complete ceasefire), they had settled down and all was quiet. From the Brigade's positions in the valley the ghostly white beams of searchlights were moving over Hum, caressing the mountain slowly as they checked for incursions from the Croatian lines. They looked like dead men's fingers.

OLIVER BURCH, MOSTAR, APRIL 1994.

REMINISCENCES

by Nerma Dizdarevic

NIGHTINGALES

The big shells were 155s and they sounded like thunder. There were also 120s and 88s. These were all fired from what we called, by the old Turkish word, *top*: cannon or artillery. We could hear the Serbian howitzers fire before the shells came down through the air, and at the beginning of the war we could actually see the flash from their muzzles on the flat-topped mountain above the town. 60s were mortar bombs, usually many landed together in the same place. Later the *četniks* had most of their long-range artillery at Nevesinje, a very poor Serbian village in the mountains to the east.

Tanks made a different sound: a double boom-boom and a quick explosion, because the trajectory is flat. It's surprising how quickly we learned about such things. The shell can punch big holes in the walls of buildings. When a tank fires at night the mountain turns orange all around with flame. HVO tanks were parked on the western hills, and at first they used to respond when the Serbs shelled from the east. We called them nightingales and we used to long to hear their voices. So many times I found myself praying: 'Please, nightingales, please,' while the Serbs were shelling and we were down in the basement. Finally they would open up — they could reach Nevesinje — and the Serbs would get the message and stop.

We all used to love the nightingales, but later, when Croats and Muslims fell out, they began to shell the Mostar Brigade on the left side of town. That was the first time I wished the nightingales would shut up.

Very often the soldiers on each side would turn anti-aircraft artillery against each other, firing tracer rounds continuously across the city from multiple recoilless barrels. The flying specks of flame look surprisingly beautiful at night, but if one of those guns is firing nearby everything shakes. Even your teeth.

I've tried to be ever so brave. Talking and going up and down and smiling at people. My husband, who was a soldier for a year, operating a rocket launcher in the front line against the Serbs, is just sitting in the room and saying: 'God take me.'

I remember one time in December, about Christmas time, the Serbs began to shell at about ten o'clock in the morning. It was sunny outside and very bright. The shelling was very heavy. One fell in the football stadium, very close to my parents' flat, and everything started shaking. So we went with all the neighbours down into the basement.

A Serbian lady from Nevesinje lived on the fifth floor at that time. She was a very simple village woman, but very nice, always saying 'Good day' in a nice way. She had two children, 4 and 6 years old, tiny little children and, like me, she was married to a Muslim who had enlisted in HVO. She was downstairs with her children, wearing a long house dress, slippers and very thick hand-made socks, the kind women wear in the villages when it is cold. Her children wore jackets and hoods, because it is always cold and draughty in the basement. She said to me: 'I was washing my little boy's hair. But I didn't have time to dry it and he'll catch cold.'

She was very frightened of the shelling. Outside all the fires of hell were burning. We had told the children to keep their mouths open to protect their ear drums from rupturing. I gave her a cigarette, and held her hands to stop them shaking as she tried to light it. And then a big *granata* came very close, and we could hear the pieces smashing against the wall outside. After one like that you cannot hear anything for a couple of minutes. You are completely deaf. Her little boy wet himself.

If anybody remembered that the *četniks* were shelling from her home village of Nevesinje, they didn't say anything. She was so confused and hysterical. A woman from the first floor, the nearest, went up to fetch a blanket for her little boy. All the faces in the basement were white and strained and everybody was smoking like crazy.

THE BEGINNING OF THE WAR IN MOSTAR

I have special memories of 6 January 1992. It was a cold day, very windy and dull. I used to have a friend who worked in a small shop down the road from my home. If I wasn't too busy, usually at about four o'clock, I would go to her shop for a coffee and a chat. She was a Serb, and didn't dislike these JNA (Jugoslovenska Narodna Armija, Yugoslav People's Army) reserve soldiers and četniks who had come to our city, but she was very careful not to show it. That day we were talking for quite a while, but all that time we never saw a soul on the street. Everything looked so empty and bleak, and because of the cold wind and the unfriendly atmosphere outside, I felt strangely nervous and tired. She told me that it was Serbian Christmas that night (the Serbs keep to the old Orthodox calendar), and that was why the streets were empty. People were afraid to walk or shop that particular afternoon.

The shooting began about six o'clock. The četniks were firing on automatic, sending whole magazines of bullets into the air. It never stopped all night. That was the first time I ever heard shooting in Mostar, and I didn't know what to do. I couldn't find a safe place in our flat. I knew that nobody was actually shooting at our windows, but a stray bullet could easily come into one of our rooms.

Later on that night we could see thousands and thousands of tracer bullets — red, green and yellow — flying up through the darkness into the sky. From my bedroom window I could see that the wildest firing was going on around the Serbian church. At about five o'clock in the morning the shooting was suddenly much louder. Later someone told us that their main Christmas mass took place in the church at five o'clock and that, in Serbia, that is always followed by a lot of shooting in the air.

I just couldn't believe that these strange men from Serbia and Montenegro, untidy with long greasy hair and beards, with at least two guns hanging on their shoulders, could have arrived suddenly and unwanted in my home town to celebrate their Christmas in such a horrible way. All that Christmas night they were singing the old *četnik* songs and it seemed so strange; songs full of hatred and their unreasonable 'call for revenge' on the one hand, and the kindly thoughts we all have of Christmas on the other.

After that the shooting came regularly, every night. We didn't know why they were shooting, but I remember that we quickly became used to it. I wasn't afraid any more, and I don't think anybody else was.

Just down the street was a little *kafana* kept by a Serb. It was named *Pretpraznićko Veče* (the Night before the Holiday) after a famous song by the Serbian writer Branko Ćopić. That was a lovely song, and Ćopić was a man who believed in brotherhood and unity among Yugoslavs, until the war came in Croatia and he decided that he believed in a greater Serbia instead. The *četniks* and JNA reservists used to gather in front of this *kafana* every evening to pass the time drinking and shooting in the air. I could see them from my window, and I used to lie in bed listening to their drunken songs until three or four in the morning.

Uncertainty, fear, and the feeling that we were not wanted in our own country any more, made us angry with the Yugoslav People's Army and with ourselves. Most of us had once had such faith in the institution of the JNA; our fathers and husbands and brothers had all served in it. Someone decided that the people of Mostar should talk to them. The Special Council for

Security was formed, and the president was the best man we had in our town at that time: Mr Roko Haskinova. He was a Croat, born and bred in Mostar where he had lived all his life, an actor in our People's Theatre, a poet and a painter. Everybody respected him, and we truly believed that he could save the situation, make people listen to each other and think, and turn hatred into friendship. We were so naïve, the ordinary harmless people of the city. We so desperately wanted everything to be normal again that we were prepared to believe anything or anybody. Even then, we could never have imagined our children under artillery fire.

A special phone-in programme was arranged on Radio Mostar, ' . . . because of the situation', they said. Representatives of all organizations, especially political parties, the police and the JNA, answered the questions of ordinary citizens. We all listened with fear in our hearts, in the darkness of our homes, unable to find any calm because the radio was almost drowned by the sound of gunfire outside.

Everybody was edgy. Nobody made the usual Mostar jokes any more. The future looked so bleak, promising nothing but worse news. The war in Croatia was the plainest warning of how it would be for us; but we also knew that if it happened to our Bosnia, which was so mixed, it would be ten times worse than in Croatia. Somehow every new morning was a relief — one more day behind us, maybe tomorrow would be better.

From the middle of February the Serbs of the city began to send their families away to Belgrade or other parts of Serbia. The departures were organized by flights of helicopters or other JNA aircraft, and they were kept as quiet as possible. But people were leaving every day, adults disappearing from their jobs and their children disappearing from school. Certain huge blocks of flats which used to be full of Serbs — officers and soldiers of the JNA and their families — were now almost empty.

All the rest of us could do was wait, and hope that maybe we wouldn't be so unlucky, maybe everybody would understand that war in Mostar wouldn't do good to anybody. People were desperately trying to relax, somehow. Some refused to listen to the news, and strictly forbade their wives and children to listen either. Some started to go fishing every day, explaining: 'I don't want to think.' Many decided to give a full service to their cars, which were out of action anyway because there was no petrol at the filling stations. In the afternoons I could see my neighbours lying beneath their cars, each with a few tools scattered around and a little chair to rest on. All they wanted to do was kill time in a way which wouldn't involve listening to the news or talking about the political situation. We were all trying to run away, for a short time at least, planning an afternoon with friends, or thinking about the coming weekend. We all wanted things to be as normal as possible. A dental appointment for two weeks ahead was enough to convince us that the situation wasn't so bad.

Our salaries had not been paid for months. Most people had no money, and the few with savings were hanging on to them. Food was very expensive, and most of the time we couldn't get much more than bread and potatoes. One big problem was that medicines suddenly disappeared from the State chain of chemist shops. If someone desperately needed antibiotics, they could only be had from private pharmacists, which were full of medicines which most people couldn't afford. We couldn't pay our electricity and telephone bills. After a time we all had quite a collection. Nobody could pay, so the power and telephone companies had no choice but to run the services free. None of these things bothered us as much as you might imagine. Any trouble, any worry, was nothing compared to the main one — war. All other troubles seemed so small and ridiculous.

Some of my friends were completely lost: with two

children, no money, nowhere to go and nowhere to hide. Our own situation didn't seem so good either.

'Let's fight them,' we would say to each other sometimes. 'Let's make a party and get drunk. Just to show them we are not afraid, that this is our town, and we have every right in the world to make a big, noisy party.'

The mood would never last. The *četniks* were making a more powerful noise, a frightening one which we couldn't overcome. Every night the sound of their Kalashnikovs was a warning.

In March life in Mostar became a nightmare. *četniks* were everywhere on the street, coming and going. They began stopping cars in the city; ' . . . checking for security reasons', they would say. It was extraordinarily annoying to be stopped in your own town, driving your own car, by some lout from Titograd, or Kraljevo, or Niš. Their behaviour was more violent than before. They wanted us to get the message properly regarding who was in charge here, and who had to listen quietly and follow the rules. One day they broke into a big shop selling wine and hard liquor, and loaded a big truck up to its roof. Many people watched the looting, but nobody dared to say anything.

We were avoiding eye contact by this time, but in the case of an accident it was safest to give a big smile. The *četniks* stopped paying for what they wanted from Mostar's shops, and the shopkeepers stopped asking for money. They were too afraid. The situation was so tense that we were all certain that war was just a question of time. And now we could literally see the big field guns on the hills all around the city. The Serbs had also positioned artillery along the road to the airport and around the three JNA barracks, all pointing towards the centre of the city. We waited helplessly. What else was there to do?

By the beginning of April people were waiting indoors, everybody keeping a bag packed ready with food and water, underwear for the children, and a spare blanket. On the 4th everything was very quiet. The next day was the Muslim holiday of *Bajram*. We couldn't even see *četniks* on the street, which was most unusual. There was a bad smell of trouble in the air. At four o'clock the radio announced that a special meeting would take place at the Hotel Neretva between representatives of all the nationalities and the JNA. The aim of the meeting was to reduce tension. We all went out to see what would happen. Soon an enormous crowd had gathered in front of the hotel.

'We won't let them come out before they make a deal,' some were saying. The big square was covered with frantic people who began to chant: 'This is Bosnia . . . this is Bosnia . . . this is Bosnia.' Nobody came out.

My husband took us for a coffee at a small sweet shop nearby. It was warm, and we were sitting outside. Many people were there, sitting or walking. We could see relief on their faces. They had been indoors for a long time, so worried and frightened, and now they were all out, walking and talking, hoping that the meeting in the hotel was going to change something. We all wanted to forget, at least for one spring afternoon, that the possibility of war was now, in fact, an inevitability. We just wanted to enjoy the smell of the spring and the feel of the city we loved so much. In the distance we could still hear the sound of voices chanting from the hotel: 'This is Bosnia . . . this is Bosnia . . . .'

The girl came out of the shop with our coffees. As she put them on the table a terrible sound began, first a cracking, tearing noise, and then a roar like a clap of thunder but very powerful, and close by, as if from the direction of the railway station behind us, getting louder all the time. As I looked around I could see the big plate glass windows of the shops along the street exploding one after another, very quickly in a line towards us, until the blast of hot air reached us and the window opposite collapsed, sending pieces of glass all over the pavement. My ears were hurting and there was a strange burning smell in the air. It was the first time I had smelt high explosive.

Everybody stood up and began to run and scream. I only wanted to find little Zlatko, who was playing in a yard down the street, to see what had happened to him. I still didn't know what the explosion was. Was it shelling? Was it an aeroplane? Why had the windows exploded like that?

I found little Zlatko running and out of breath, his face red and his hair full of slivers of glass. I told him to keep his mouth and eyes shut. And when I turned back I saw my husband with his wallet open, ready to pay for the coffees. Everybody else was screaming and running, and the waitress was nowhere to be seen. I was very annoyed with him because, in such a situation, he looked so silly waiting to pay for coffees we never touched, on a table covered with broken glass.

We went home immediately and I cleaned the glass out of Zlatko's hair. From the window of my bedroom I could see a lot of black smoke from behind the railway station. We were waiting for the radio to tell us what had happened. The neighbours were leaning over the window sills, craning to see something which might explain that horrible explosion. After half an hour we could see many people packing suitcases into the boots of their cars, and whole families leaving, escaping somewhere.

'Croats,' I thought to myself, 'or Serbs.' Croats could go to western Hercegovina; Serbs could go to Nevesinje, or other places in eastern Hercegovina. But we Muslims could go nowhere.

At that moment I panicked, and couldn't stop crying for a long time. Then I smoked for a while. Finally, Radio Mostar told us that a big tanker lorry had been packed with explosives and parked in front of the JNA barracks behind the station, which was full of četniks. Someone had detonated it by remote control, and the damage was appalling. More than a hundred četniks had been killed and many more wounded in the barracks, and at least ten civilians living in the block of flats opposite were dead. Later we heard that Croat extremists had planted the bomb.

At first it didn't make sense to me. The *četniks* were ready to start the war anyway, and this explosion, or any explosion, would not stop them. Now that the Serbs had so many dead and injured, they were full of anger and completely determined to begin their war which they had been planning for so long, and in such detail. At that time I didn't understand Croats as well as I do now. It never struck me that the Croats of western Hercegovina were even more eager to begin the war in Mostar than the Serbs.

The following night was the longest of my entire life. I wanted to go to the right bank, to stay with friends or my parents in the other part of the city. It was a safer place to be at that moment, but my husband didn't want to go. We were very nervous, arguing and shouting at each other, and all we could hear was shooting from outside. I could see soldiers running up and down the main street with guns, and firing occasionally, but not in the air. I put little Zlatko to sleep in his bed and packed all my things in two travel bags. My husband was sitting down watching television, but I was too nervous. So I roasted a chicken from the freezer and made a lot of biscuits in case we had to run away. The sounds from outside were terrible. In the darkness of that night I heard hand grenades for the first time, and men crying out after being injured on the street.

In the morning the street was quiet and empty, except for two men in front of the shop down the road waiting for the baker's van. With the last of my money I bought two large loaves, a big salami and a small, hard cheese. People were talking about the fighting in the night. It seemed that the JNA and some local men had their 'eye contacts' at last, and opened fire on each other, even throwing bombs.

'It's not going to be all right,' they told me. 'They killed two soldiers.'

I put all the food in separate bags, dressed little Zlatko and gave him some breakfast.

'I am going to the right side now,' I told my husband. 'If you want to come with me, that's good. If not, I wish you luck.'

He came with me, and we left our home forever. I never spent a night there again, and I no longer think of it as my home. There are a few things I miss: my piano, some photographs, the Turkish carpet my father gave me. Soon afterwards I ran away from Mostar for the first time.

BABA JANJA

You make mistakes in wartime. There are always moments you regret.

I remember that there was this old Serbian lady called Baba Janja who lived on the third floor of our apartment block on the left side. Although she was old, 75 I think, she and I had coffee together a couple of times every day, and we shared all our cakes. Every cake she made, she would give me half, and I the same. I always gave her the best presents I could afford for 8 March, Mother's Day. Her attitudes weren't old. She treated me like a daughter.

Baba Janja looked after little Zlatko when I had to go to school early in the morning. I would make a coffee at seven o'clock and light the stove to make the kitchen warm. Then I would knock on the floor with something, because she was underneath. She would come up to knit and drink coffee, and I could go to work. Little Zlatko would still be asleep.

When the war started, I left Mostar. My husband looked after Baba Janja, because she was a Serb and her position was difficult. By the time I came back, our flat on the left side had been wrecked by *četniks* and we went to live with my husband's parents on the right bank. But I wanted to see my Baba Janja immediately. After that I would go to visit her sometimes with a pack of coffee or chocolate that my brother got from the Red Cross. She didn't have any water to her flat, which caused her a lot of trouble. The whole left side was without water right through the war, because the pipes under Tito bridge had been destroyed. My brother couldn't understand our friendship because of the age difference, and he used to tease me: 'You can't live without your old Baba Janja.' But really I loved her very much.

Once, when I went over to my flat on the left side to try to clean it up a bit, she was there on the floor below. When I finished cleaning I went down to drink a coffee with her, and she asked if I would take her across the old bridge, because she wanted to visit some relatives on the right side. Old Janja couldn't see too well and it was a very bright sunny day. She couldn't manage without thick glasses and she wasn't too good at walking uphill, which she found very difficult. So she needed someone to help her over Hairudin's Bridge, which was the only way across then.

We left, walking very slowly in the direction of the Old Bridge because she couldn't walk fast. I remember that she was talking about how expensive onions were. I don't believe that she was really so worried about onions. It was just one of those subjects people used to seize upon to avoid feeling lost during the war. One got very depressed talking about the real situation. It would always be easier to talk about onions: whether they were expensive, or whether they were not.

When we came to the open space before Hairudin's Bridge we found it packed with people. A man was selling sugar that had certainly arrived in Bosnia as humanitarian aid. Some people still became very angry when they saw aid being sold in a market. But this man looked very poor and, who knows, maybe he had a bunch of children at home? He had about ten kilos and he wasn't selling in a shop. He wasn't a

Mostar man, but probably a poor Muslim from some place like Nevesinje which had been taken by the Serbs. I decided to buy in this case. I didn't really need sugar at the time, but I bought two kilos to help him.

Then Baba Janja and I climbed up to the top of the Old Bridge. Ever since I was a child, I always used to stop for five or ten minutes on the top of the bridge, just to enjoy the view.

While we were on the top, the Serbs suddenly started shelling. We heard the siren start and I saw smoke from the first shell on the right side, somewhere near the medical school. Everybody was running to get off the street. If the *četniks* shelled the old town, you had to run because there was no shelter. All the small houses were destroyed without any roofs. You couldn't find protection there.

The top of the bridge was a very dangerous place, about as exposed as it was possible to be. But Baba Janja was so frightened that she couldn't move at all. She wouldn't budge. I held her arm and said: 'Please, just try.' And at that moment the second shell fell on the left side by the Armija, close to the flats we had just left. We could feel the Old Bridge shake a bit under our feet.

But Baba Janja still couldn't move. She was so frightened she just sat down on the bridge where she was. People were still running. Some soldiers at the end of the bridge were shouting at us: 'Are you crazy? Come off there.' She wouldn't move; she just sat there. I was very nervous and frightened. I couldn't help it. I have never been so frightened. I said: 'I can't stay up here.'

She answered: 'Then go if you cannot stay.' I wouldn't, couldn't go, and leave her. But at that moment another shell landed very, very close. I could feel the heat. Sometimes, if a shell is close enough, you can feel the heat and smell the hot metal. I heard pieces of smashed *granata* and glass striking around us, and the Old Bridge really shook.

I found myself running down the bridge to the right

bank, and turned off to the side where there is a little shop with a roof above the steps leading down to the river. Some people were standing or sitting inside, and someone said that we were all crazy because the shop didn't make much of a shelter. One piece of *granata* could smash the whole flimsy building.

Old Baba Janja was still sitting on top of the bridge, quite unable to move. After a couple of minutes we couldn't hear any more shelling, and I lost the feeling of being frightened. You know how it is with fear; you just get it, and then you lose it. Nobody understands why. When you lose it you aren't frightened even if the enemy is all around you.

So I climbed up the bridge again to where the old lady was sitting alone. She made such a sad picture, sitting there in her fear. Baba Janja weighed about 100 kilos and I knew that I could never move her. I felt so ashamed because I had left her there alone. She said: 'You cannot run away from destiny, if the shell is for you. If God meant that *granata* for you, you cannot run from it. So why try? If it isn't for you, you don't need to run. If it is for you, then you can't escape.'

That was her very simple philosophy.

I offered her a hand and asked: 'Can you get up now?' She didn't want to take my hand. She got up herself, holding on to the stone parapet of the bridge. After that it took more than an hour to reach her relatives' house. She carried on talking about onions and such things. That was the last time I ever saw Baba Janja. I left her there, and I never saw her again though I managed to visit my flat on the left bank a couple of times.

I still feel ashamed about what happened on the bridge. When you are as frightened as that you just run. I didn't think.

BLAGAJ

When I was little, early winter mornings would begin with the smell of wood smoke from the new fire. My grandmother wouldn't want me to get up too soon, because it took quite a while for the house to warm up. Outside I would hear her making butter out of milk in the traditional way — churning the milk very hard in a tall narrow pot with a stick which was flattened at the end. Later she would walk in with a small jar of butter. The room would be full of the lovely smell of the fire and home-made bread, and she would give me my favourite breakfast: freshly churned butter on a piece of warm new bread and a cup of milk. I always had that feeling of being at home with my grandmother. The warmth of home was everywhere, in the old cooker and the wood fire, in the bread, milk and butter, in my grandmother's friendly face as she tried to warm her hands at the hearth. I couldn't have enough of that one room in the old house by the mosque in Blagaj. I could forget the whole of the rest of the world.

My grandfather, the butcher, would be outside in his shop, and we would hear customers talking to him. Sometimes he was in a good mood, but usually he was shouting: 'Get yourself a chicken! Lamb is not for you!' This was for customers who wouldn't buy a larger piece of meat, or not large enough for grandfather's liking. It was only his loud voice, and nobody was annoyed with him. Everybody was used to it. His temper was him, my grandad, a butcher.

The population of Blagaj was mainly Muslim, but there were Serbs and Croats in the village as well. The main street was not more than 200 metres long, but first you came to an Orthodox church, then a Catholic church, not as old, but very gothic and rather pretty, and then the mosque where my grandparents' house was. All the churches in a line, all on the same street. People never had any problems about nationalities in Blagaj, and they lived very happily together. Can you believe that some mornings you could hear the bells of both churches ringing and the singing of the *imam* at the same time? It was more tuneful than you might imagine.

I used to go back to Blagaj to stay with my grandparents during the summer holidays. When I was only 14 I managed to convince people that I was serious enough to hold down a job in what we called the Turkish House, actually a *tekia* or monastery, which the village was so proud of. All I had to do was serve coffee and smile at the visitors, but I was dressed in traditional clothes, with an embroidered blouse and head-dress, a broad belt with silver clasps, and wooden shoes. I looked like a girl from the past, just as everything in that lovely old Turkish House was from the past. It was all wooden, with carved walls and banisters on the stairs. There was one large room downstairs, with a large bright Turkish rug and handmade furniture with cushions on the divans. At the centre was a low table with a machine for making coffee — made of metal with little holes for a fire and a stand where the big *ibrik* of coffee stood, always hot and ready. In my country, drinking coffee was a ritual which went on for hours, while people took their time discussing serious matters or problems. Copper ashtrays were everywhere, and little metal plates for *lokum*, which is a sweet usually served with coffee in Bosnia. If it was morning there would be baskets of figs on the table because figs are supposed to taste best at the very beginning of the day, before coffee or anything else.

The room upstairs looked similar, but on the floor were the coffins of three Muslim saints, and an *ibrik* of water stood by each coffin to refresh each holy man. According to legend the good saints protected the village and its people, and the fact that the water in the *ibrik* was always gone after three days was a proof of their power.

Visitors would usually enjoy their coffee and *lokum*

in the garden of the *tekia* at wooden tables, sheltering in the shade of an ancient oak tree, with the freshness of running water below. The source of the little river Buna, which was so charming and green and full of trout as it made its short journey to the Neretva, was just behind the Turkish House. But the spring itself was a very mysterious place, where an enormous amount of cold green water came welling out of a dark cave. Nobody would ever swim or fish in that sinister pool, but only stare into the depths, or at the strange black birds which flew in and out of the cave. The source and the pool were at the bottom of an enormous cliff which hung out over the water so that you could not see the top where the eagles had their nest, although the great birds could be seen gliding out across the fields. Somewhere up there, too, were the ruins of Castle Hercog from which Hercegovina got its name. Further down the stream was the mill, which was always turning, and smelling of new flour in the mornings. When I remember these things, it seems to me that I must be mistaken. Blagaj seemed like a piece of paradise from some ancient time.

The village was usually very quiet, except twice a year when dervishes from all over Bosnia made a pilgrimage to the *tekia*, to pray and chant beneath the saints. These men in Turkish days had lived in monasteries and were very influential. Only the rich could become dervishes. But now they had no power, just a fanatical faith. They wore white scarves tied round their heads, and brought their wives and children on the pilgrimage. They would pray and meditate on a single subject together, sitting in a circle in the main room of the *tekia*. After a while they would sink into a trance so deep that they would begin to pronounce strange animal-like sounds, like the barking and growling of dogs or wolves, gasping all together, faster and faster. Then some would take skewers and pass them through both cheeks. There was never any blood. The proof that God accepted them, and was near to them, was that there was no pain and no blood. It was rather frightening for me, but I would be very busy afterwards serving hundreds of coffees. At the end I would always be given a towel and soap, the traditional gift for a young girl.

My grandparents were married for more than fifty years in all, and were never apart for long. He looked after my grandmother, but not in a gentle, loving way. He would provide everything she needed, and then disappear for a few days, usually fishing. He had asthma, and needed to be out in the fresh air. Much later, when he had bad days and felt really sick, hardly able to breathe, he would call her name all night long. It wasn't enough that she was sitting on the bed, holding his hand.

My grandmother died first, of cancer of the blood, and in great pain. At the end she did not forgive him certain moments of cruelty, or his habitual blasphemy in swearing by God's name. My grandmother was a very religious woman and I remember that the last month of her life was the month of *Ramadan*. People were not supposed to eat before eight o'clock, when the lights were lit on the minaret. Every day there was a doctor waiting for the lights to show from the minaret so that he could give her an injection of morphine, the only pain-killer which could help her. She died on the first day of the *Eid*.

My grandfather was desperate and died very soon afterwards. My uncle and his family lived with him at the time. Grandad was always calling for my grandmother day and night, screaming through the window. He would not accept that she was gone.

After grandfather died the dream of my childhood was broken. Blagaj and the old house by the mosque were never the same. I gave up my summer job at the *tekia*. I was 18 by then and decided to leave as well, to keep Blagaj as it had been, strong in my memory. I rarely went back.

One day in April 1992, at the beginning of the war, I

heard that a line of a dozen tanks from the Yugoslav People's Army went into Blagaj. When they reached the Orthodox church at the beginning of the street, they found all the Serbs of the village blocking their way. In charge of them was the priest, Papa Skočojić, with his wife and three military-aged sons. The Serb commander in the first tank stopped, and Papa Skočojić said to him: 'You only go through this village over our dead bodies.' There was an argument but the priest was adamant and they had to turn back. The Serbs held the mountains all around and close above the village, so that you could see them, but the people continued their lives there together. I don't know how the later war between Muslims and Croats affected the village, but I hope not much. Someone worked hard in my country to spoil the warm feelings people had towards each other in such places as Blagaj.

HATIDŽA

When my uncle Sulejman was about 18 years old, he met the girl that was to become his wife. He saw her when walking through the village of Gubavica on his way to Nevesinje. Gubavica is a very poor village, because the soil is sandy and only good for grazing sheep. My aunt Hatidža was washing the family's clothes in the stream when Sulejman saw her. She was never beautiful, but Sulejman must have seen something about her that attracted him. She was just 14 years old.

My uncle walked straight up and stood above her on the bank and asked: 'Would you like to marry me?'

And without any hesitation or shyness she replied: 'Yes.'

So Sulejman took Hatidža by the hand and led her back to my grandfather's house at Blagaj. When they reached home, my grandmother was milking a cow in the stable. Sulejman called to his mother to come out, but not too loudly because he did not want his father to hear. He was afraid of my grandfather and his temper, as everybody was in Blagaj. My grandmother Aziza eventually came out to see what Sulejman wanted.

'I've got married,' Sulejman whispered. 'This is my wife.'

He whispered because he didn't want my grandfather to hear. He was always upstairs, and he had a very bad habit of listening to other people's conversations through the window. But my grandmother was deaf, and she hadn't heard what Sulejman said.

'What did you say,' she asked. 'Tell me again.'

'That's his wife you old fool!' roared my grandfather from the window upstairs. 'The idiot has got married.'

He asked Hatidža her family name. When he heard it, he said: 'I know them, I know them. A bunch of gypsies and vagabonds, but what difference does it make now?'

Of course Sulejman and Hatidža were not properly married under Yugoslavian law. She was only 14 years old. But according to the custom of the villages in my country, the fact that they had walked away together was enough. They belonged to each other now, and Hatidža was Sulejman's responsibility. Her parents didn't make any problems about it; Hatidža was the youngest of twelve and they were grateful to be rid of her.

Sulejman said to my grandfather that night: 'Do you want us to sleep in one room or two?'

'If you came together, you had better stay together,' he replied.

Hatidža was pregnant almost immediately, and her first son, Mustafa, was born when she was 15. She helped my grandmother around the house at Blagaj, looking after the cows and cleaning and cooking. I was 10 at the time, only a few years younger than Hatidža, but she was already a woman. She was always very kind to me.

Sulejman was messing around like an idiot. He

72

worked as a labourer, but he never kept a job for long. He couldn't always manage to arrive at work on time. He was always disappearing for days at a time, drinking or womanizing, although he already had a wife and son. My grandfather used to talk to him, trying to explain that he had responsibilities now, and that he must keep a job. Nobody had forced him to get married, but now he had to take the consequences. Sulejman went on just the same and my grandfather grew angry: 'One day I'll cut your throat from ear to ear. You know I can do it.'

During the winter holidays while I was staying with my grandparents at Blagaj, Sulejman disappeared for three days. My grandfather said: 'I've had enough. I can't take this any more. When he comes back, that's it.'

After that, everybody was very quiet and gloomy waiting for Sulejman to return. A *bura* was blowing and it was very cold outside. I was sitting on the floor, rocking little Mustafa in his cradle, when my uncle finally walked in. My grandmother was in tears at once, expecting a storm when her husband came down.

I will never forget how my grandfather looked when he flung open the door from the stairs. All my life I have always admired powerful things, fierce things like eagles and wolves, and that is why I remember so well how he looked that day. My grandfather was a tall man, not fat. He was too nervous and irritable to be fat. He had very dark thick brows and deepset eyes, and he always wore a black beret and a long black greatcoat thrown like a cloak over his shoulders. He was asthmatic, but extremely strong from his work as a butcher and he was famous for being able to hold and slaughter a bull single-handed. He was almost always angry about something and people were afraid of him, so he spent most of his time alone. If everything was well in his shop, he would leave his servants to look after it and wander about the country, dynamiting trout or casting nets for them in the Buna, even in the middle of winter. He didn't need the money; that kind of illegal fishing amused him.

Hatidža and I got up immediately, to show respect, as we always did. He sat on a chair and caught his breath for a moment, so that all we could hear was the rasping of this breath and the moaning of the wind outside. Then he said to Sulejman: 'Didn't I tell you I would cut your throat from ear to ear?'

Everybody was quiet and my grandmother quickly slipped between them. Then my grandfather pointed at Mustafa and said: 'Now collect your little bastard and your wife and all your stuff. You have two minutes. Anybody I find here after two minutes is dead.'

Then he went back upstairs.

We all started scampering about the room like mice. I helped Hatidža to collect the baby clothes and put all her things in a suitcase. She wrapped little Mustafa in a blanket because it was so cold outside. And then they were gone, all three of them. I saw them going down the *socak*, two figures cuddling a baby in a blanket. My grandmother was desperate, crying in real pain, telling my grandfather: 'I'll never forgive you for this, not even on my deathbed.'

She was serious. Muslims are supposed to give *halal* at the end of their lives, forgiveness for whoever has done them any evil, but she wouldn't forgive this. It seemed too cruel to her.

Sulejman and his family stayed in Mostar with my parents that night, and soon after that they found a room in the city. When Hatidža was 16 they got married with a letter of permission made out by a lawyer for her parents to make a mark on. They stayed in Mostar for some time, but their life went up and down, accordingly as Sulejman behaved or misbehaved. With another baby coming Hatidža had a bad time of it for a while. Sulejman was always chasing other women, sometimes bringing them home and making his wife cook for them. They were just cheap prostitutes, but what else could Hatidža do but put up with it? She had nowhere else to go. But sometimes, when she couldn't take it any more, she would bring her children to my mother's flat for a couple of days.

After some years, in his own good time, Sulejman calmed down a bit, and my grandfather bought them a cottage in Blagaj. My uncle and his wife and children began to function as a family at last. Mustafa, and Enver the second son, were both nice boys, although Enver was very mysterious in some ways. When they started school Hatidža learned to read and write from her own sons. Hatidža was not an attractive woman, but absolutely devoted to her family. There was one thing about her that everybody had to admit: she knew that she would have to ensure that her children had enough to live on, because her man would always be unreliable.

She found ways to make money. She would rent large plots of land and plant spring onions, with only her boys to help. From the age of about 8, Mustafa and Enver were both working in the fields with her. When the onions were ready she sold them to the government co-operative in Blagaj. She used to keep about thirty hens, and sold the eggs every second day, sometimes walking all the way to Mostar to get the best price. She used to climb the mountains around Blagaj, collecting wild herbs to sell for cooking or making tea. If there was nothing else to do, she would walk about the country collecting firewood, so that when the winter came she would only have to buy a cubic metre of logs to heat her house. Everybody else needed five metres. She was like a goat, very tough and brown, always out and always working hard.

When times became really hard in Yugoslavia, the roles in our family were reversed. The other ladies in our family, so clever and pretty with their fair skins and university degrees, couldn't handle the difficulties which came to everybody. But Hatidža could. She was tough. When the wind blew all the tiles off the roof, she would be up there fixing them back. The other ladies, large or small, were so delicate that they would never consider ruining their soft hands by picking onions, or so timid that they would never consider picking herbs on the mountain. Perhaps for fear that a poisonous snake might bite their tender and shapely behinds!

By that time Hatidža's hard work had paid off. She had changed. While we were suffering and wondering how to make our salaries stretch, she would come round one day in expensive leather boots. Or she would take a taxi to the station, which we could never do. Suddenly she seemed a very interesting person, and everybody wanted to call at her house, to ask after her and see how she was doing. People were so anxious to drink coffee with her. But she remained cool; she knew exactly what was going on.

When my grandfather died, he left his house to his second son, Smail. But Smail was already rich, with a big flat in Mostar and a house at the seaside, so he didn't have any use for the old Turkish house in Blagaj. He told his brother Sulejman to move in. So Sulejman and Hatidža with their two boys moved in and looked after the house.

When it was obvious that Sulejman and Hatidža were becoming quite well off, Smail suddenly decided to sell the house because he needed the money. It wasn't kind, but it was his right. He went to Blagaj and found Sulejman in Čaršija, which is the street where the shops are, and said: 'I've got something important to say to you and your wife. Can we go to the house?'

When they were all sitting together inside, Smail began in a very serious tone: 'I've got my personal problems, and I must tell you that I have to sell this house. I decided on a price and I have already advertised once in the Mostar newspaper. And I nearly found a buyer.'

Apparently the man was a Croat from Podveležje, who had come back from working in Germany. He had liked everything about the house except for the fact that one wall was attached to the mosque. So Smail was fairly sure that he would be able to find another buyer at his price before long.

Hatidža asked: 'Well, how much is this price of yours?'

'15,000 German marks,' said Smail.

Hatidža said: 'Wait a minute, please.'

What happened next seemed unbelievable, even to those who saw it with their own eyes. Hatidža went upstairs and came down with 10,000 marks which she put on the table in front of Smail. Sulejman had never known anything about it.

'Here are 10,000,' Hatidža said. 'Give me one month and I'll have the rest of the price for you.'

So Sulejman and Hatidža stayed with their children in the Turkish house at Blagaj with its old-fashioned furniture and its yard and stable. From that time Hatidža was treated with the greatest respect by everybody in my family.

MEDUGORJE — THE HOLY CITY

Before 1984 Medugorje was one of the poorest villages in western Hercegovina, mainly inhabited by old people, sheep and goats. Tourist guide books didn't mention it. Hardly anyone had heard of it. But in June of that year a group of children picking wild strawberries claimed to have seen the Madonna in the sky above a nearby hill.

The local press got hold of the story at once. The news came to Mostar via the radio station and even the Croats of the city were cynical about it. But Croats from all over western Hercegovina flocked immediately to the place until the roads were blocked for kilometres around Medugorje. For a week nobody could get in or out because the crowds were so great.

In Medugorje's little church a special mass was held to which Cardinal Kujarić of Zagreb and a number of Croatian politicians were invited. The circle of praying people extended for a kilometre around the church. The original group of children appeared so often on television that people knew their names by heart. They described the Madonna as having worn a grey veil and a pale blue dress, and how beautiful she was when she smiled at them. She had told them that she would return every day for a while.

The masses continued. Contingents of fervently religious Italians arrived, and of course the Irish. The children were given important places at every mass and prayed as if in a trance, longing for the return of the Madonna. On top of the hill where the Madonna had been seen, a wooden cross was erected. Some pilgrims decided to climb the stony hill barefoot, in order to suffer as much as possible on the ascent. Their feet would be cut to ribbons. Often television cameras were ready for interviews on their return: 'How was it? What did you feel?'

In Mostar we saw the children interviewed again and again on Croatian television, revealing more and more of what they had seen and heard. They were always announcing that the Madonna was coming to make another visitation — two days later at four o'clock in the afternoon, for example. Everybody would be on their knees ready at that time. Once there were 100,000 kneeling around Medugorje. But nobody could ever see the Madonna except the children. And people knew they were seeing her because they went into a trance. They were chosen.

After a month or two the Catholic authorities decided to change the timetable, so the Madonna didn't show up again. It was all too inconvenient. The children were taken off to a monastery somewhere in Croatia to be given a religious education. They were chosen, after all, and they would grow up to become priests and nuns. Their families did pretty well, one way or another. They didn't suffer.

When everybody had calmed down a bit, they started to build hotels and motels, cafés and bars.

Almost overnight the little village of Medugorje, which had no tarmac road before, began to grow. Instead of the miserable wooden cross, they put a huge concrete one on the Madonna's hill.

Medugorje became such a popular place. Every festival, fair or show, celebrating anything material produced in western Hercegovina, was now held in the village. Something was always going on. Fairs for honey-makers, wine-makers, tobacco-curers, ham-smokers, sweet-bakers, or anyone else with a product to sell, were all held there. The Madonna got her share too. All the products of the earth were left under her cross, and the nuns had to be very fit to keep climbing up and down the hill for cheeses, hams and bottles of wine. All year they were up and down like Speedy Gonzales, collecting stuff to be distributed around the different churches.

Meanwhile the population of Medugorje was making friends with the foreigners who came to visit the holy place with their dollars and Irish pounds, especially those who were foolish enough to come two or three times a year. In the local newspapers we could read of the friendships which grew up between villagers and rich American ladies who came time after time to stay in the same family homes. They were such touching friendships. American Catholics were always regarded as the most important group, then the Irish, then the Italians. New flights to Zagreb were laid on from the United States and Ireland, and the pilgrims were brought on by luxury coaches. A hundred thousand came to the first anniversary of the Madonna's appearance.

Some in the Catholic Church kept their heads. The Bishop of Mostar refused to believe in the miracle or to have anything to do with what was going on at Medugorje. He lost his job over it and was so disgusted that he left the Church altogether. I heard later that he was a shoe-repairer in Zagreb and much more content, he said, than he had been as a bishop. The Pope and the Vatican declared that the events at Medugorje had nothing to do with Catholicism. But that had no affect on the devout Catholics of western Hercegovina. At Medugorje new blocks of houses were springing up like mushrooms, without any kind of urban planning, so that the place began to look like a frontier town in the Wild West. It seemed that nothing could halt the economic miracle of Medugorje.

THE RANCH

I could never imagine my father as a retired man. He was a very hardworking person, but more important than that, he had his pride. He had to feel important, like someone who can't be replaced. Very often people from his agency telephoned in the middle of the night, asking if he would go to one of the mountain villages near Mostar to clear the roads of snow. He was always ready to go, feeling very happy. Or if they needed some new machine collected from Ljubjiana, he would be on his way to far-off Slovenia in his lorry in five minutes, telling us: 'I don't know what they would do without me' — pretending to be annoyed but, in fact, very happy.

After his second heart attack he didn't feel strong any more, and began to dread the time when he would reach retirement age. An old dream of owning a small weekend house somewhere in the country close to Mostar, came into his thinking more and more.

When my mother's father died at Blagaj, the dream became a possibility. My grandfather, the butcher, had been a rich man, and all my uncles inherited land in the village and money. I was left a cow. My mother got a little shop on the village street, which she sold, not for very much, but it was more than my parents had ever had in their lives before. This was my father's chance; he made a deal with my mother's brother Sulejman to start building them both a house in Blagaj, on the beautiful place we call Baćak. It seemed a wonderful idea. My uncle had inherited the land from my grandfather, and my father would supply the materials and do the building work. My uncle would give my father half of the land as a present. At the finish they would each own a small country cottage side by side.

I had spent a lot of my childhood at Baćak, which still seems like a piece of paradise as I remember it. There is a little river of green water surrounded by fields, and a hill covered with grass and small bushes. The fields had belonged to my grandfather, who never grew vegetables like everybody else, but used them to graze his cows, because the water was in the middle of the property and the grass was of the very best quality which could be imagined. The thousands of red poppies which appeared on those fields in spring inspired me to write my first song, which won first prize in a competition. The prize was a week at the seaside near Makarska for my family. We never went because it turned out that food wasn't included and we couldn't afford to pay for that at hotel prices.

My father began work on the cottage. He forgot about his road maintenance agency. His job as a driver wasn't the most important thing in the world any more. Night after night he couldn't sleep for thinking about his house. He had to build a little road first and dig the foundations, which took several months. Everybody helped him: his friends from work, his brothers and all our family. My mother was cooking for all these people. In Bosnia, if you ask someone to help you with work you are expected to feed them afterwards. I was often there serving food with my mother. I remember my father's face — happy, proud, healthy and sober. For the first time I could remember, we didn't worry about him at all.

At first my mother and father were spending the money she had inherited very cheerfully. It wasn't a fortune, the equivalent of about five thousand English pounds, and because it was being spent on a house they had no need to feel guilty. But they weren't used to such wealth, and perhaps because she didn't really understand how to deal with such a lot of money, my mother began to feel that something was wrong.

And she was right. My famous uncle Sulejman, probably influenced by his wife, broke his promise. It suddenly emerged that he didn't want his share of the double property after all. He didn't want his house, and he refused to sell half the land to my father or to make a present of it to him. So my father had to stop work. He had to leave the little road he had just built and the new foundations and everything else.

It was like the end of the world. We were very quiet. Nobody would say a word. Everybody was so disappointed. I spent hours in the apartment waiting for my father to say something. He just sat on the floor, staring at one point in the pattern of the old Turkish carpet. My mother sat by him, smoking, and when it was time for a meal or coffee, she would give me a sign to serve it. Nobody wanted to eat, but we had to, just to make the situation seem normal. We could hear the clock and my brother's steps up and down in the corridor. My father was so sad and his pride was injured. What would his brothers and friends say when they heard of the disaster? I knew exactly what was on his mind. He was old-fashioned in that way, as in many ways. And I was worried for him. I worried that he might have another heart attack.

For some time the situation remained unchanged. The money was gone and my father's dream destroyed. Some of his family were quite happy about his loss, so complacent. People are always jealous of other people's success. And when something goes wrong, they are suddenly so very understanding, often visiting, even though it wasn't their habit before, and talking about trivial things. Deep inside they feel pleased. I hated them. And so did my father.

I had just got married at that time, and had a little money in the bank remaining from my wedding gifts. I desperately wanted to do something to help my father.

So I managed to find a piece of land in a village close to Mostar where one of his brothers had a little house. I went to see the Serb who owned it, asked if he was willing to sell and, if so, how much he wanted. To my surprise, I had just enough money to pay for it. When I had all the papers in my father's name, I gave them to him. He refused to go and look at the place; he was so embarrassed and angry. But we made him go. There is an old custom in my country that pregnant women must be humoured. I told him: 'I am pregnant, so come with me.' It was quite true, although he hadn't known it till then.

So we went to the village of Lakiševine together. He was so pleased, because the property was only 300 metres away from his brother's house. It was a nice village, but short of water, without any river or stream. That was a bit disappointing and something I hadn't considered when buying the land. But later we found water underground on my uncle's land and I persuaded a friend to send an irrigation pump from Germany, so that both properties had all the water they needed.

My parents spent most of the next seven or eight years at that place. We all called it 'ranč', as if it were an American ranch. My father began to build a lovely house while my mother grew all sorts of vegetables. They couldn't talk of anything but their ranč. It wasn't easy, because they had to pay their workers and for the materials. My brother and I helped as much as we could. I paid for the roof out of my teacher's salary, and many times cooked meals for the workers to help my mother. My father knew a builder called Salko who came to do the skilled work. We called him *Maestro*. He was a very short-tempered man, but good at his job. We bought an electric cement mixer from a Croat friend of mine in one of the western Hercegovinian villages. But however my father and brother mixed the sand and cement and gravel, the result was never quite right for Maestro Salko.

The ranch was the only bridge between my father and I. Whenever I saw him I would ask him about it, and he was always happy to talk about the building work, if nothing else. And so my parents, after all the years of pain, were happy at last with each other and their ranch. Even while the men were building, my mother was planting all sorts of vegetables in little patches. Everything in the garden was so tidy, planted with a string to keep the lines straight. She put in flowers, too, all varieties of flowers carefully placed in order, blue, yellow and red, and again blue, yellow and red. It was all perfection. There was work and back-ache and strain, but such happiness. She enjoyed this pleasure for five years in all.

To tell the truth, sometimes I couldn't understand my parents. After spending all weekend at the ranch they would come home, have a bath, and then a coffee. Over coffee they would talk about nothing but what they had done at that ranch from Friday to Sunday, every detail, on and on, until the rest of the family had heard enough. But we all knew that that was the first time they had spoken the same language, one which only they could understand, and one in which they could enjoy each other. That's why that ranch was so precious. They finally lived together as one. And they lived for Fridays.

On Sunday evenings they would come to my apart-ment with a basket full of peppers, tomatoes, parsley, carrots, potatoes and onions. Later, in autumn, there would be sugar melons and grapes. They were so proud of what was in that basket. My father would sit down very carefully on my sofa, which was almost white, saying, 'I was in my garden all day long, maybe I am not clean.' I knew that he was clean, but he liked to say that he had been in his garden, especially if visitors were there.

I always laughed when one of my friends came to see my father's ranch at Lakiševine for the first time. He was so very happy to show off his house.

'Look,' he would say as he opened the door of the bedroom, 'it's dark inside, but if you want a light you just press this button and switch the light on.' So few houses in that village of poor Serbs had electricity. Or in the bathroom, 'You use the toilet and there's no reason to be embarrassed. You just pull the lever for the cistern.' It was so hard to organize running water in that village. The visitor from the city would be mystified at what all the fuss was about, but we took care to laugh only when my father couldn't see.

It became a tradition on the first of May for the whole family to dine at the ranch. We would roast a lamb, as Bosnian people do when they want to celebrate. And the party would last all day and all night, through the holiday into the second of May.

My brother married about that time, and he lived with his wife in my parents' flat in Mostar. My father and mother moved more or less permanently to the ranch. They and my uncle were the only Muslims who had ever lived in Lakiševine. The villagers simply adored my parents. They were such kind and good neighbours to them. For his part, my father helped them build a road into the village and repair the Second World War monument they were so proud of. He gave them water, lent them tools from his workshop, and shared everything he had to keep their friendship. No doubt he had in mind that they were Serbs. By that time the tension in Mostar itself was becoming very obvious, and many people in the city were afraid of the Serbs.

One day *četniks* from Serbia and Montenegro came to Mostar and the nearby villages. Nobody would call the soldiers and reservists by that name because it was too dangerous. They claimed they had come to protect the helicopter factory, but from whom, nobody knew. Maybe from the citizens of Mostar who worked there. They would walk along the streets of the city with loaded rifles, untidy, loud and unfriendly. Lakiševine was full of them, because the villagers couldn't wait to offer their hospitality. The dream was gone for my father, and it was replaced by fear. It wasn't easy for a Muslim to live in a village full of Serbs and četniks. His brother left immediately, but he decided to stay, whatever happened.

The day came when četniks burnt my uncle's house. That was terrible for my father. My parents were at their ranch all the time, being very hospitable, my mother making meals and coffee for četniks. They were treating the house as their own, using the bathroom, sleeping everywhere, eating, drinking. In Mostar we never disliked the Serbian people of Montenegro, although we used to make fun of them sometimes for being lazy and a bit slow. There was a joke about a Montenegrin radio announcer: 'Good morning, working people of Montenegro; it's twelve o'clock, time to get up . . . '

Some of these soldiers in the village were very nice: young men who didn't really want to be there. They were missing their families and some had young children. But most were very abrupt, loutish men, and never separated from their guns. It was awful for my father, but he thought that the situation could not last for ever and at all costs he must save the house.

About this time my Serbian neighbour Draga had a telephone call from her sister in Titograd, the main city of Montenegro, to ask if her son was all right. This boy Vukoslav was a četnik, so of course he was all right. It was more a question of whether he had killed anybody yet, but a mother couldn't be expected to see that. Vukoslav was supposed to be in Lakiševine, where my father's ranč was.

Although my father had told me to stay away from the village while the četniks were there, I went with Draga on the bus one afternoon to ask after Vukoslav. From the bus stop we had to walk up a steep path, the short way to the village. We couldn't see anybody about, just a couple of goats. Draga was big and fat, and couldn't go fast. She was complaining all the time about how steep it was.

Suddenly at least two rifles started firing ahead, not at the path, but into the long grass on either side, about ten metres away. There was a tremendous noise and I could see the grass kicking crazily.

When you hear something like that you just have to run. You can't possibly understand if you haven't experienced it yourself. I didn't think about Draga; I just ran up the hill to the houses on top. I realize now that it wasn't serious shooting. The sentries on the hill above the village were just having fun. Later on it seemed very funny, but at the time I was frightened. At the top of the path I waited for poor Draga to catch up.

At the beginning of the little village street was a small *kafana* owned by one of the Serbs in the village, and the yard was full of real *četniks* lounging around, the first irregulars I had ever seen in the flesh. Here they were with their long beards and greasy hair, some of them with big silver crosses on chains around their necks. They looked just as they did in the old photographs. They were sitting on little benches and on the wall around the *kafana* or lying on the ground. They all had guns in their hands, or slung over their shoulders, or on the table beside them. One had crossed belts of machine gun ammunition on his shoulders.

Draga said to them: 'God bless you, my heroes.' which is a popular greeting in Montenegro.

And they all replied: 'And God bless you too, lady.' But they looked at us very closely because we were new faces in the village.

We went on up the lane to my father's *ranč*, and we met *četniks* everywhere, standing around talking in groups, lying outside every house, in the yards and behind the fences. At that time there were more than a thousand *četniks* camped in the fields around the village. We could see field guns on the hill, pointed in the direction of Mostar. Everybody stared at us.

When we reached my father's yard I could see that something was very wrong. The white gravel which my father used to rake so carefully every time he saw a mark in it — even when little Zlatko was playing out there he used to follow him around with a rake — was now churned up by lorry tyres and hundreds of boots. That would normally have seemed unbearable to my father.

On the table in the porch was the fruit press which my mother used to crush plums for making jam. It had been used, but days before, and now it was covered with flies. My mother was very tidy about her things, especially on the *ranč*. Outside the door was a long row of Kalashnikovs leaning against the wall: maybe twenty of them. No shoes, as is the normal custom in Bosnia when guests are polite, but just rifles.

I knocked at the door and we went in, Draga still out of breath and puffing. Inside were my mother and father playing hosts to a house full of *četniks*. They were sitting on the sofa, the arms of the sofa, and all available chairs. *Četniks* would never sit on the floor inside a house as we would; they think that is Turkish. When my father saw me he got up at once, very shocked. He signed to me with his hand to get out.

'I'll be with you in a minute,' he said loudly to his guests. And quietly to me, 'Get out quick.' He was very angry and his face was white.

I was outside in a moment, trying to explain why we had come. The *četniks* had followed us, one by one, and were listening to everything we said. But my father was too frightened to concentrate on what Draga and I were telling him about this young boy Vukoslav. The *četniks* were listening with great interest, but they didn't speak.

My father told me to get into his car and he would drive me down to the bus stop on the main road. Draga wanted to stay, but I didn't have a choice. In the end she got into the car with us, not knowing what else to do. The *četniks* watched us leave as my father drove down the hill, telling me how stupid I was, and what a difficult situation I had put him in. He was right. At that moment I understood the real situation and was very sorry that I had caused him more worries by coming.

After that, right until the end, the *četniks* came to my father's house all the time asking about his daughter. When would she be coming back? Was she married? Who was her husband and where was he? What was her address in Mostar, and what was the telephone number? He told them that my husband was a physical training instructor at the JNA pilots' school, but they persisted in asking him questions.

The *četniks* had free run of the house during the day while my father was at work. My mother would cook plenty of food for them and leave for Mostar. They would help themselves to baths and anything they wanted. Eventually my mother stayed in Mostar because she couldn't take it any more. But my father was determined to stay. When he came home from work he would spend the evening pouring drinks and making coffee like a very happy host with a house full of friends. If they broke a glass or left the ashtrays full, it didn't matter. At ten the *četniks* had to report for evening roll-call at the camp in the field across the road. My father would breath a sigh of relief, thinking that he had seen the last of them at least until morning, and that he had saved his house for one more day.

One cold night he heard the sound of a big truck pulling into his yard, and then a lot of shouting and laughing. He got up and saw that *četniks*, all very drunk, were falling out of the back of the truck and staggering about the yard. He opened the door of the house before they broke it down.

At this moment his neighbour Đorđe came from his house across the street. Đorđe and my father were very good friends, always drinking coffee together. He said to my father, 'Look, Adem, it's not safe for you here any more. We can't protect you. Please go home to Mostar. Don't worry, we'll look after the house.'

My father knew that he really had to go now. He was terribly afraid and went straight with his car keys to the garage and workshop beside the house. But some of the *četniks* were not quite as drunk as he thought. One of them said to him: 'No, no, old man. Just leave those keys here. You can go on foot.'

All my father saw on the roads were JNA trucks full of *četniks*. He walked all the way to Mostar, in the early hours of the morning, humiliated and afraid, knowing that he had lost his *ranč* and his car.

Two days later the real war began with the Serbs in Bosnia and we had enough to worry about in Mostar. That was when we all learned about artillery, rockets and shells: 88 millimetres, 120 millimetres and 155 millimetres. Maestro Salko, our builder, was one of the first victims. He was standing in front of his block, Omladinska Building Number Seven, a tall one with eleven floors. The shelling had been going on for a while and there was nobody on the street, but for some reason he couldn't stay inside any more. A shell hit him directly as he stood on the pavement. His body was scattered all over the place, in pieces. His wife saw it. She always looked from her balcony on the sixth floor to see where the shells landed. It was a sort of game she played. My father told me later that Salko's body was all over the bushes in front of the block. His daughter escaped to Spain later, before the Croat-Muslim war.

When the *četniks* were chased away from Mostar and the villages to positions on the hills around the city, my father went to his ranch, frightened to death that he would find it destroyed. But the Serbs of the village really had looked after his house before they ran away. Everything was as he had left it. He couldn't stay for more than five minutes, but long enough to put his name on the front door.

It was fortunate that he did, because later on the HOS (Hrvatske Oruzane Snage, Croatian Armed Forces) came to the village and destroyed everything except my father's house. HOS were Croatian fascists, men who would do any dirty job, commit any obscenity in the name of their race. They hated Serbs. I remember them so well in their black shirts with swastika badges, their skull and crossbone emblems and their Nazi salutes.

After a couple of weeks my father risked another visit. The village which had stood for over a hundred years had been destroyed. The houses were blown up or burned out; all the wells and cisterns were broken and the water poisoned; his neighbours' gardens were burnt; the cattle wandered around half wild with hunger and thirst. Everything was destroyed. Only his own house, identified by his note on the door as the only non-Serb house left in that place, was untouched, just as it was.

My father was defeated. He surrendered then. My father, who had very nice handwriting, carefully wrote another note and put it on the door. I have seen a photograph of it which my brother developed later at the Red Cross office in the city. The note read:

'Please HSO, do this one too. When my neighbours come back, when I see them building houses again, then I will build mine. This is not my house any more.'

My father was crying for days and days. Later, when the war had already lasted for more than a year, I told him to cheer up and that I would pay for the roof again when I had the money. He smiled and said: 'It's going to be the White House this time. Just wait and see.'

BELGRADE

I spent the first two weeks of the war in the basement of my parents' block of flats. At that stage we didn't know what the Serbs wanted. They were shelling most of the time, but more often at night, and the *granatas* were not aimed at the city, but falling on the hills around. We heard that there were Croats up there as well as Serbs.

After twelve days the Serbian commander told us on the radio that someone had kidnapped two JNA pilots. If they didn't get their pilots back unharmed by four o'clock that afternoon they would start shelling the city. Everybody knew that the story about the pilots was one for little children. And exactly at four o'clock they began to shell the university.

I didn't know what to do. The problem was that I had no money. Serbian friends who had run away to Belgrade were telephoning and inviting me to join them. I knew that I would be able to stay with them without money, but how could I get there?

That night in the basement I talked to Ankica Davic, a lady from the second floor. She was a Serb, and very frightened and quiet. I told her I wanted to go to Belgrade, but I didn't know how to get there. Did she know anybody who could help me? She said she knew a helicopter pilot and could call him. So we went up to her flat and reached him by telephone. Ankica asked him to help me, and he agreed, saying that I should be at the heliodrome next morning.

When I told my husband he was against the idea as always, and we had the usual argument. But next morning I was ready to go. I checked that all my papers were in the bag, dressed little Zlatko and gave him his breakfast. It was quiet outside. My mother and father, my brother and my husband were all sitting drinking coffee. Only my husband knew that I was leaving.

I announced that I was going to Belgrade, and I wanted to say goodbye. There were only two minutes left for talking, and they were all completely shocked. They were looking at my husband, expecting some kind of explanation from him. But I had to go.

My husband drove me to the airport. He knew many people there, having worked in physical training at the pilots' school for so long. Now the days of instructing young airmen in skiing and swimming were forgotten.

Instead we found a huge crowd of people, almost all of them Serbs, waiting for a place on an aeroplane or helicopter. We had to park a long way from the heliodrome and walk. Everywhere were military policemen with big alsation dogs, which always frighten me. Finally we reached the terminal and looked for the pilot I was supposed to meet, but it was impossible. There were so many people pushing and shouting and waving papers that we couldn't even get into the building.

We gave up and I smoked a cigarette, trying to think what to do next. My husband was very worried and confused. So was I, but I knew that I had to think carefully. After a while I saw a familiar face. It was a man who used to be our neighbour, a Serb called Srdan Dašic, and I called out his name. He explained that his wife was coming in five minutes by helicopter from Sarajevo, and then she was going straight on to Belgrade. If there was any room for little Zlatko and me, he would try to put us in.

The helicopter was down in five minutes, right on time. Srdan had told me to watch him; if I saw him waving with both hands to run out to the helicopter. The rotor blades were still spinning and people were coming and going. That minute seemed like hours. Then suddenly I saw Srdan waving and I took little Zlatko by the hand and started to run. The helicopter made a lot of noise and wind as we got in. It was up immediately.

Srdan's wife Sanja was inside with her two children, and she told me that we were going to Titograd first, and then later to Belgrade. That didn't worry me, as long as we were out of the war zone. The vibration from the engine was so strong that our cheeks were shaking and little Zlatko was sick all over me. I hardly noticed at first, because I was so interested in what I could see from the windows. We were flying low, close to the tops of the mountains, and everywhere I could see trenches, soldiers and howitzers. I remember a field kitchen and soldiers sitting eating on the grass of a meadow. Further back there were lorries and tanks lining the roads all the way to Nevesinje. Fortunately we came into Titograd airport in just half an hour.

As the airport was full of *četniks*, I asked my friend if she would kindly call me by some other name than my Muslim one. She said, 'OK, Milena.' So I became Milena, and told Zlatko that his name was Jovan. Maybe we didn't have to do that, but I was very frightened to see so many *četniks* around us. Some of them were ordinary JNA reservists, very young and tidy, but most were real *četniks*, smelly and unclean, with long beards and dirt under their finger nails. They were talking quite openly to each other about the terrible things they were doing in Bosnia. I pretended not to hear.

My problem was that I had no food for little Zlatko, who was very hungry. It was late in the afternoon and the airport was about fourteen kilometres away from Titograd. A very young soldier was smiling at me. He was going into town, and I asked him if he would be kind enough to buy us *čevapčići* or something like that. Later on they put us all in a big room to sleep. The room was used as a hospital and there were twenty beds in it, some of them occupied by wounded soldiers. I slept on one bed with little Zlatko, and my friend on another. Her children wouldn't keep quiet.

The soldier was back with the kebabs at about ten o'clock. Little Zlatko was asleep, but I woke him up to give him some of the food. I gave the rest to my friend's children. The two of us stayed hungry.

Early in the morning they gave us black coffee and the children some biscuits in the waiting room. There were no telephones working, although I wanted to call my mother and father. I knew they must be worried about us. After a while some soldiers told us to go and wait for the helicopter at field number 18. So we began to walk there. It was about eleven o'clock. I was tired and hungry and my shoes were making blisters on my feet. Little Zlatko was anxious about the helicopter and if he would be sick again.

The helicopter came in at four o'clock, full of JNA officers. They all disappeared in the direction of the airport building, leaving only the pilot. He said that they would be back in half and hour, and also that passengers from Titograd wanted to go to Belgrade, so there might be a problem about weight. If we were too heavy he wouldn't be able to lift the aircraft up.

My friend Sanja showed the pilot a piece of paper and she was allowed to put her bag and her children inside. Zlatko and I were left outside with some other people, still waiting for permission to get in. The officers came back and climbed inside. Then the pilot told the rest of us that he was very sorry, but he had a full load.

I was too frightened to panic, and I asked the pilot if he would listen to me for just two minutes. Fortunately he said: 'OK.'

I told him quietly: 'Listen, I'm not a Serb. I am Muslim. I don't know exactly where I'm going. But I've got this child with me, and if you have any children at home of your own, please don't leave me here. I can't stay here with these soldiers. It's too dangerous. So please take me somehow. Please.'

He looked at me for a moment and I couldn't stop the tears. I hadn't wanted to cry. But suddenly I felt so frightened at the thought of staying another night among all those *četniks*.

Then he said, 'All right, get in. I can jettison some fuel to lose weight if I can't lift it. I would rather do that than leave you here. And I have two children at home.'

I was so grateful to that Serbian pilot. I could tell he had some problems getting the helicopter to lift, but once we were in the air he turned round and smiled at me. In Mostar people used to say, 'We don't claim that all Serbs are *četniks*. By no means. But the problem is that all *četniks* are Serbs.' I knew very well that this young pilot was no *četnik*. I will never forget his proud, smiling face looking at me after he lifted that machine up with the engine shaking and vibrating. One Serb and one Muslim communicating quietly in extraordinary circumstances. It takes so little for people to be able to understand one another. How could we ever be at war?

Zlatko was sick again on the way to Belgrade. The helicopter was so crowded that people were sitting on the floor. This time I was ready with plastic bags and handkerchiefs; but we had no fresh air. The helicopter was going up and down all the time, changing height every two minutes. I was very worried about my son because he looked as if he were about to faint. One of the officers told me not to worry. It was quite usual, because he wasn't used to flying.

After two and a half hours we were at Belgrade. The pilot told me that he was going to drop me off at the stadium, right in the centre of the city, so that I could easily catch the bus or a train. I couldn't believe what I was hearing. And right in the middle of the football stadium Zlatko and I were off, just the two of us. We watched the helicopter lifting again, waving to the pilot like crazy. When it was high above us, we saw his hand waving back.

I phoned my friends, and two hours later they came with their car to take us to Kragujevac, where we spent the next three months. Everybody was very nice and friendly, but I decided at the beginning not to discuss politics at all. And I stuck to that decision. We knew very well that we didn't have identical opinions about certain things, and if we could accept that fact we could go on for a long time without problems. We made jokes, went for long walks over lovely country-side, had meals every day at three o'clock, and we played cards in the evening.

I was among friends that summer. That's how they made me feel.

'Nerma is like a cat,' my father used to say. 'However you throw her, she always lands on her four legs.'

I am famous for that. I always swim, never drown.

LJUBLJANA

You can be a guest in somebody's house for just so long. After three months I knew that we would have to leave Serbia. We would have to be refugees from the war somewhere nearer home, perhaps in Dalmatia. Perhaps it would even be safe to go back to Mostar soon.

A bus line was still running from Belgrade to Ljubljana, despite everything which had happened. But the tickets were expensive, and I couldn't expect my friends to help with money. They didn't have any themselves. For a couple of days I was under pressure about what I should do, thinking very hard.

Then I remembered that my husband once had a friend who was now quite a well-known doctor in Belgrade. I remembered his surname was Posarac and found it in the telephone directory. One evening I phoned him. Believe me, it is very difficult to ask for money from a person you have never met. But I really didn't have any choice. I told him my name, said something about my husband, and finally asked him if he could help me. There was a long silence from the other end. Vlada Posarac probably needed some time to remember my husband at all. Then he answered that he would help me, and we arranged to meet in Belgrade.

I went to the city with little Zlatko and Vlada waited for us at the railway station. It was a bit difficult to find each other because the station was big and crowded, and of course we had never met. But he had told me on the phone, 'I'll wear sun glasses and I'll have a little girl with me.' I didn't have any sun glasses and I had a little boy with me, so we recognized each other after some time.

First he took me to his flat, where his wife Saška was waiting with lunch. It was a wonderful flat, very modern, full of glass and metal furniture, and I was quite happy following them around to see all these lovely things, until we came into the living room. On the wall was a huge painting of Mostar's Old Bridge. After a moment I burst into tears. I just sat in front of the picture, shaking and sobbing, quite unable to stop. This unexpected sight of 'the Old One' was like the touch of my mother's hand.

Vlada and Saška left the room and quietly closed the door. Of course they understood. I was frightened about such a long, dangerous journey with my child. I was embarrassed to ask for money from people I didn't know. I was tired. I was homesick. And then, at the end of everything, this beautiful painting of my dearest bridge, which to Mostar people means home and the warmth you can find only at home, had made me feel so lost, yet at the same time impatient to leave. All the beauty of the Old Bridge and my home was in front of my eyes, but still so far from me. They didn't even try to comfort me.

Later they explained that the painting of Hajrudin's Bridge was a present from Vlada's friends when he finished university. Had I forgotten that Mostar was his home town?

'Me too!' was all I could say, trying not to cry again.

Then after lunch they told me that they would buy the bus tickets for me for the following Friday. We spent the weekend with them and their lovely little daughter Ana, and then went back to Kragujevac. The week passed very quickly; I packed our bag again, and my friends kept saying how worried they were about us. We had a small goodbye party on the Thursday. They bought roast leg of lamb and a lady made a wonderful cake with strawberries. Everybody was so sad, but not me. To prevent myself being frightened or worried I had convinced myself that I was really going home again.

Next morning we took the midday bus to Belgrade. Vlada and Saška and little Ana were waiting with a nice present for Zlatko, and we all went to have lunch in a pizza restaurant. The Ljubljana bus through Hungary didn't leave until eight o'clock in the evening. Zlatko was feeling particularly happy: 'I'm lucky not to be going by helicopter this time,' he said.

I began to feel very nervous. At twenty minutes to eight we were in front of the bus station. I put our bag into the bus, which was very old and dirty, and Vlada gave me the tickets and 100 German marks. The marks were such a relief, because I didn't have any money at all, as usual. Finally the noisy, worn engine started, and we began to move. I could see little Ana waving and Saška cleaning her glasses with a tissue.

It was still daylight. The bus went very slowly through the streets of Belgrade and after a while we reached the motorway. Zlatko was very tired and fell asleep almost at once. I was quiet and still nervous. 'Who are all these people going from Serbia to Slovenia in wartime?' I asked myself. They looked like businessmen. Everybody looked very serious, and I tried to find a friendly face. No luck.

The countryside was wonderful. Endless flatlands covered with corn and sunflowers, green and yellow, without any trace of a hill. The sun was disappearing far away and everything around us was slowly sinking into darkness. I asked myself what fortune such a night might bring to the pair of us.

My passport was the old Yugoslavian type, but Zlatko's was Serbian. He had not had his own papers before, so I had taken one out for him in Kragujevac. These documents were good for Serbia, but likely to cause trouble later. I was uneasy and my stomach began to ache.

After a couple of hours the driver took a break. We were about 100 kilometres from Subotica, the Serbian town closest to the Hungarian frontier. I started talking to a frightened lady who said she was carrying a Croatian passport, and was expecting trouble on the

Serbian border. I gave her a cigarette and an orange, and showed her my own papers.

'Don't worry about this border,' she advised me. 'Your problems are going to come later.' That made me feel even worse.

We continued our journey and Zlatko fell asleep again. I was too nervous and worried to sleep. Before long the bus stopped again and the lights came on.

'Serbian border,' the driver said.

I could hear my own heart beating. Three policemen came in. They took our passports, stamped them, and just smiled at me. But there was trouble as soon as they saw the other lady's Croatian passport. They took her off the bus. While we waited, I looked at the Serbian stamp, a cross and four cyrillic letter 'S's, in each of our passports. 'This won't help me,' I thought.

The Croatian lady was back, crying and under arrest, to collect her bag. She tried to speak to me, but the policeman was too close. She was gone again in a moment.

I wondered what she had tried to tell me. What would I do if something like this happened to me? I was completely helpless in this bus. The journey was like a nightmare.

The Hungarian officers let us all pass without any problems. The drive through Hungary was a period of calm, because I knew we were safer now that we were out of Serbia. I wanted to calm down and think carefully again. Instead I fell asleep, and when I woke up I ate an apple. It was a very uncomfortable bus, but I made the seat space as cosy as I could for little Zlatko. He was fast asleep, and looked like a very smart boy lying on my lap. I felt furious that policemen and soldiers were ready to frighten children, whatever papers their country had given them.

After three hours' driving the bus stopped in what seemed to be the square of a little town. There was some monument in the middle which I couldn't see properly in the darkness. The Slovenian bus was already waiting for us. As soon as we were seated in the soft seats of this almost new, luxurious bus, the driver switched on his tannoy and said something like: 'Good evening. We are very happy to welcome you, and we wish you a comfortable journey on to Ljubljana.' Then, almost as if it were an afterthought: 'If any passenger is travelling on a Serbian passport, we would advise them to leave the bus here. We would remind you that Serbian passport holders are not permitted to enter Slovenia.'

Zlatko's Serbian passport seemed to be burning a hole in the pocket of my jacket. I went forward to explain the situation to the driver, and he said: 'Try it. You might be lucky.'

Maybe I had worried for too long or maybe I was just tired. I fell asleep, completely relaxed. The bus was comfortable and warm, and I was happy to float along through the darkness without anything on my mind. I was going home, and I would get there whatever happened.

The bus stopped again at daybreak, and I woke up to see a border post. But which one?

'Hungarian,' someone said. Of course they let us go, but the next one was Slovenian. I was ready. Worried but ready. Two Slovenian officers came in and I waited for them to work their way along the bus. This time the other passengers were all producing their second passports from their inner pockets: Croatian, Sloven-ian, German, Italian — anything which didn't link them with the country from which they had just trav-elled. I gave my two passports up to the officers, and the taller one, with a big moustache, looked at me and said: 'You've got no chance.'

On the way back down the bus he told me: 'Leave the vehicle. You can't enter Slovenia. You'll have to go back.'

Go back? I followed him, holding little Zlatko by the hand. He told me to wait in front of a small office. Through the window I could see him leafing through

our passports, telephoning somebody. Then I remembered that my husband had a Slovenian friend,
and that I had the man's first name and telephone
number. Unfortunately I couldn't remember his surname. I knocked on the door and started to talk.

'Excuse me. I only want to pass through Slovenia. I
have no intention of staying here.'

'That doesn't make any difference.'

'I've got a friend in Ljubljana and he'll be very cross
when he finds out how you treat a woman with a
child. This used to be my country too, you know.'

'What's his name?' the officer asked.

'Igor,' I said and gave him the telephone number.

'What's the other name?'

'I don't know.'

'Forget it. Look, go and get your things from the bus
and go back.'

'What do you mean, go back? To Hungary?'

'I don't care where you go. Just do what you're told
if you don't want to have real trouble.'

We were both shouting now, and little Zlatko was
crying. It was just 4.30 in the morning. I knew that
there was no hope, but I wouldn't shut up. Not with
my big mouth.

'Look, you Slovenian officer, you think you are
doing a great job here. I'll manage, you know, but I just
want to say that I hate you. That's a personal obser-
vation you know. One from me to you. And I want your
wife and child to be in some trouble.'

He was very angry. 'Get lost before I put you under
arrest. You're all gypsies and thieves anyway. All you
Bosnians.'

'Well you are not! Thank God you are not!' I shouted
back, and trailed off to collect my bag. I must have
looked very funny. In a couple of minutes the bus was
gone and I was left alone with little Zlatko, still crying,
with my bag on my shoulder. And then the same
officer was back again.

'Just go away,' he said. 'I don't want to see you here again.'

I didn't want to argue any more. But I couldn't believe how my country had changed. I had been to Slovenia so many times as a schoolchild and later, as I grew up. I had never needed any kind of passport. Slovenia was so beautiful, like one great park, and I had been proud of it because it was part of my Yugoslavia. The people were a bit cold and selfish, but the scenery was adorable. And now this man was telling me to go away, at 4.30 in the morning on the border.

I walked back to the Hungarian side and approached the border officers there. They were kinder and more friendly. I had to hand in the passports, but I could stay for a while at least. I needed time to think, to decide what to do. There was a little shop, like a kiosk, on the border crossing, which was already open. The Hungarian lady there very kindly offered me a coffee and Zlatko an ice-cream. It was weak coffee, without milk, but I was very grateful. Later she gave Zlatko a big bar of chocolate.

I was waiting for something, anything, to happen. I wasn't going to panic. I couldn't change the situation. I tried to stay calm and smiled from time to time at Zlatko. It was a very cold morning, so I found his jacket in the bag and made him put it on. He looked much better than I did, very cheerful, desperately trying to charm the lady in the kiosk into giving him another ice-cream.

Halfway through the long morning I noticed a fellow in a red car with Slovenian plates driving towards me, very close, and then slowly reversing back again. He kept up this strange forward and backward business for some time, and I became fed up with watching it. If he wanted something why wouldn't he say?

'Excuse me,' I asked him, 'can I do something for you, or are you just practising driving your car backwards and forwards?'

He got out of the car then, and asked, 'Do you want to go to Croatia?'

'No,' I answered. I like it here. If I had any chances for breakfast I would never leave the place.'

'I'm serious. I can drive you there.'

'OK, what does my part of it involve?'

'100 German marks a head.'

'100 is all I have. If I put my little boy on my lap, can we still go for a hundred?'

He smiled and shook his head. 'No way. I treat all my customers the same.'

He was about to drive off when I remembered something.

'Hey, Mr Moustache Man (because he had a very big moustache), if I give you 100 marks and all my rings, will that make you happy?'

'Show me the rings.'

I gave him my left hand, on which there were four rings.

'OK. You pay immediately and get in the car.'

First I asked the Hungarian border officers for our passports, and said in the nicest possible way, 'Thank you.' Then I gave the man 100 marks and the four rings, and we got into his car. This man could have been anybody. I was very nervous, but I didn't seem to have a choice.

We drove back along the border towards Croatia (the borders of all three countries meet near Lendava), while the man talked all the time. He had a wife and three daughters. His life was difficult as far as money was concerned, and that was why he 'had to do this', as he put it.

'I am a decent man,' he said.

'Of course you are,' I had to say.

He showed me a photograph of his family: a pleasant-looking lady with two girls of about 5 and one small baby in a push-chair. I almost felt sorry for him, and I did feel that I trusted him.

We passed through the Croatian border without any

difficulty at all. I am certain that he worked with the officers there, because he spent some time talking to them and shaking hands. After half an hour we were in Varaždin bus station.

The man told me to destroy Zlatko's Serbian passport. That could cause us big trouble in Croatia and he could manage without one. There was nothing to be done about the Serbian stamp in mine. He wished me good luck and gave my boy a kiss. And then he was gone.

I had no idea what to do next. But then I saw him coming back with his red car.

'I've got to ask you something. How are you going to get anywhere without any money?'

I was so touched. Suddenly he looked so friendly and understanding.

'OK,' he said. 'Because of the boy, you understand, take 30 marks from me. It's because of him, not you. You aren't my type anyway. You smoke too much!'

I could only say thank you and take the money. Then he smiled. 'I'm joking, but you do smoke too much.'

And then he was really gone.

I was so pleased with the situation and feeling rather proud of myself. I really don't know why, because we had been lucky. I've done it! I kept thinking to myself. The night before we were in Belgrade, and now we were 100 kilometres from Zagreb. Who can do this? Only me!

Many people could do it, but I was trying to make myself feel better. I had done it alone with little Zlatko, and I wasn't frightened or harmed. I managed to get through. I went into the ladies' toilet, burned Zlatko's passport with my lighter, and flushed the ashes down the pan.

Later on we took the bus to Zagreb and telephoned Igor in Ljubljana. My husband had told me he was a kind man. He drove across the border to meet us in Rijeka, where he gave me some money and bought us bus tickets to Split. However, he warned me against going back to Mostar, where the situation was still very bad.

Igor, little Zlatko and I went out for a drink before the bus left. Igor was talking about his job and how his daughter was going to France for a holiday. The coffee bar was big and empty. I was worrying about Split. I had no idea what to do when I got there. But Split was close enough to Mostar, and I knew I would find plenty of refugees there. Someone would tell me.

Igor had a bag full of fruits and sandwiches and sweets for us. He was a very kind man, and he looked very serious as the bus was leaving. He was not so much sad as worried, although he told me not to worry. We both knew that I would be in danger on the road to Split. That part of the coast was checked very often by soldiers and irregulars, especially at night. I didn't want anybody to see the Serbian stamp in my passport, but that was the only document I could show at the checkpoints.

The bus was full of Croatian families and HVO soldiers (The Bosnian Croat Army). A lot of children and babies were crying all night long. Zlatko was soon asleep, although I promised to wake him when we reached the ferry at Pag. I was eating oranges and trying to talk to someone. But nobody was really interested. Maybe it was because it was very late and there was no fresh air inside the bus. Everybody was a bit nervous.

At the ferry we went outside. Zlatko was very excited by the ship and the sea, and the hot wind was pleasant. I smoked a cigarette very slowly, trying to relax. After some time we were back on the bus; Zlatko soon fell asleep again and I was just about to. Everything seemed to be usual and normal. I didn't mind the babies crying, somebody's bad smell in the air, or any other unpleasant sensation. I just wanted to get to Split. Nothing else was on my mind. Nothing else was important. I couldn't see anything outside, but I knew that part was pretty dull, no houses or trees, just the dark, empty road going on towards Zadar.

Suddenly the bus stopped and the lights came on.

'Could you have your documents ready to be checked please,' the driver called. Three men with black uniforms, black hats and black ribbons tied around their foreheads had come on board. They were slightly drunk. The most frightening thing about them certainly wasn't the AKM rifles on their shoulders, the pistols and handcuffs at their waists, or their shiny leather jack boots, but the mark on the uniform — HOS.

HOS was an organization of fascists, a nightmare left over from the days of Anti Pavelic's puppet Croatian State during the Second World War occupation. Their sacred heroes were Mussolini and Hitler. They were fanatics, and they hated everything Serbian. I have to say that many young Muslims joined HOS in Mostar at the beginning of the war, mainly because it seemed to offer them a good chance to fight back against the Serbs. HOS didn't hate Muslims, but what would happen when these three saw the stamp in my passport? They were coming towards me.

I was in the middle of the bus, waiting, knowing that there was nothing else to do. I looked down at little Zlatko's face, which seemed so beautiful as he slept. I was beginning to shake, thinking what would happen to my son if they killed me now. Would they kill him as well?

'Identity card, please,' one of the blackshirts asked me.

I gave him my passport and a big smile. He smiled back, swaying slightly in the aisle, opened the passport, saw the picture and the name, and Mostar as the home town. Mostar was on the front line, being shelled by the Serbs, and that was probably enough for him. He closed the passport and gave it back to me.

'Good luck,' he said.

After that moment life was so beautiful for me. All my worries seemed to be behind me. I gave my boy a kiss and tried to make myself more comfortable, hoping to sleep. I was on my way to Split and nothing was going to stop me now. I wished that someone could have been there beside me at that moment, someone to whom I could have told the story of how close it had been, although I didn't even want to imagine what would have happened if the soldier in the black shirt had turned the next page of my passport and seen the Serbian cross. It was all behind me now.

The bus was on its way to Split, driving very fast. The new day was just about to break, and I decided not to sleep after all. The coast was beautiful. The sun coming out from behind the hills produced a pale glittering on the sea, which then grew slowly more and more blue. Small boats were drawn up on beaches and a big white liner was sailing far out on the horizon. A yellow plastic ball lying on the sand had probably been forgotten by some child the night before. Two fishermen were setting their lines. Then we came to the first houses of the big city of Split. It was 5.30am.

The bus station was empty. Zlatko was a bit cold after sleeping on the warm, cosy bus all night. I left him sitting on a bench while I looked at the timetable board. I was searching for somewhere small we could go to, preferably closer to Mostar. Then I saw the name *Podgora* on the board, and I remembered that it was a lovely village by the sea with a charming harbour. I decided to go there.

Two hours later little Zlatko and I finally left the bus on a lively corner of Podgora's main street. I was holding his hand, and the nearest hotel looked so pretty.

'Shall we try this one, Zlatkić?'

The car park was full, and nearly all the cars had Mostar number plates. It was a wonderful sight. The

Hotel Mediterranean was to be our home for the next five months.

PODGORA

The hotel had obviously been very nice before it took refugees in. There were six very long single-storey buildings, so that the rooms and apartments looked like small bungalows, each with a little garden. Just perfect for a package holiday on Yugoslavia's beautiful Dalmatian coast! My room was number 209, and the garden had a white table and three chairs. It was in the shade for most of the day, and was a good place to pass the heat of the early afternoons. The reception office and restaurant were in a separate building where we went three times a day for meals, or, if we were lucky enough to have some money, to make telephone calls.

All the women had to work every day. When I arrived the administration wanted me to work in the kitchen. There was a shortage of electricity to run the machines, so the main work was washing up. Most of the rest of the time I was peeling potatoes. It was hot in the kitchen and extremely smelly. To be quite truthful the smells were not connected with the food being prepared, but with unwashed, sweaty clothes. Some of the women in the kitchen were from remote, primitive villages in Bosnia and Hercegovina, and many of them from the dry mountain districts around my home town. People in such villages rarely have enough water, and they don't believe in wasting it. To wash themselves every day seems to them an unreasonable thing to do, even when they find themselves in a hotel with plenty of soap and water, and the adorable Adriatic sea just below the palm trees across the street.

The time I spent in that kitchen was difficult for me. I just couldn't take it, and once I fainted. All I was dreaming of was the fresh air and clean sea water beyond the door. I decided to be useless in the kitchen to ensure that they threw me out. And they did. The boss told me that he was sorry, but I was so unsuited to the work and so distracting for everybody else, that he must ask me to leave. He didn't have to ask twice. They found me another job, but fortunately that was outside.

I was very short of money. In fact when I first arrived at Podgora from my jaunt around five of Yugoslavia's republics I had none at all. The obvious solution was to find a good friend among the women. Someone for whom I could do something, and in turn get something. The circumstances were sharpening my mind. I was beginning to think as a refugee must in order to get by. I wanted someone interesting, or interesting enough to go through this long boring summer with.

It didn't take long to find Željka. She was a Croatian girl from Bugojno, tall, slim, very dark-skinned, about 26 years old. She had a gypsy face but a nice clean smile. She was totally without education, very common and loud, with the exaggerated, insulting sense of humour which is typical of that part of Bosnia. The only defence against such humour is to behave in the same way. She made her own jokes. Most people can't do that. Her clothes were fantastic: outrageously short skirts and only a funny little T-shirt on top so as to leave her tummy naked. I really liked Željka. She had her own original style, unconventional, but in many ways right for our situation. She was a good survivor.

All the other women, mainly from small villages, found Željka disgraceful, and gossiped about her all the time. She amused herself by trying to shock them as much as possible. Her little daughter, aged between 2 and 3, was very sweet, but was never washed. She looked like a tiny hungry animal, desperate to wolf down any food she could possibly find. Tina with her big blue eyes was eating constantly, anything she could get her sticky little hand on.

Željka only had boy-friends. She was against marriage. 'They are better in bed when they are only boy-friends,' she used to say. She didn't claim to love her boy-friend, Tina's father, but she needed him, once a fortnight, for sex in return for which she received money.

Tina's father was a big guy belonging to HOS, a *mafioso* with a lot of money. It was said that he had seventeen children by eight or nine different women. He was a generally bad character; later, someone shot him in a bar somewhere in central Bosnia. More than likely an angry husband. Every time he was around Željka had a bath, gave me little Tina to look after — 'If I hear her crying, you are dead' — and shut the door of her room. The other girls and I would sit outside laughing. Often the door would open after a couple of minutes, and there Željka would stand in high heels and wonderful underwear the boy-friend had brought her from Germany, lacy hi-cut panties without any behind in them, and stare at us with a very cool, serious expression.

'Quiet, please. I need some concentration, OK?'

We would all start to laugh again, and all we could see, while she was closing the door, was the silly little face she made: 'Don't you envy me, ha! ha!'

After a couple of hours her boy-friend would leave and she would be teasing us again: '400 German marks; what do you say? Don't worry, girls, your husbands are coming soon and you'll get lots of figs and grapes and tins from Caritas. Just take it easy.'

I looked after Tina a lot, and in return Željka looked after me and little Zlatko. She never bought only one bar of chocolate, or one of anything. Tina and little Zlatko always had the same. We shared everything, the good and the bad, in a delightfully open, friendly way. Željka moved into my room, and her room was for fun — for cooking, smoking and parties. We kept our room clean and tidy, and when the children were asleep sat listening to music or telling each other our life stories.

Željka's childhood had been very tough. She had never known her father. Her mother, whom she loved very much, had supported her by working long hours cleaning people's houses. She had never experienced such simple pleasures as a family Christmas party. Her mother was all the family she had, and she was working too hard to spend much time with her. Željka grew up by herself, learning by her own mistakes, which is always very difficult, but a good school for wartime. As a grown-up she was determined to show that she could live her own life without listening to anybody who had ideas about what was good or bad for her. When I realized that she was only such a tough character on the surface, but listened to people she liked with a softer, inner part of her mind, I tried to stop her being alone so much. She listened to me and I was flattered.

Our long, boring days were based on the beach. Mornings were the time to enjoy the clean water and the sun; later it would be too hot to be out of the shade. We would swim by turns, so that someone was always watching the children. About eleven o'clock Željka would buy a sugar melon and we would eat it just before lunch. After we had eaten enough we would give the rest of it to children from other parts of the beach who had gathered around waiting. They were refugees and didn't have enough of anything. Then Željka would take them all for an ice-cream. It was a regular sight to see the tall figure of Željka, her thin brown body revealed rather than concealed by a shocking pink bikini, and twenty children of about Zlatko's age, all disappearing inside a sweet shop.

We ate lunch in the restaurant with the other refugees. People of all ages, many of whom had never left their villages before, came in and sat down, waiting patiently for the meal to be served. Their sad eyes often showed a complete absence from the present time and place. They desperately missed their homes, which many of them would surely never see again. They would stare at the white table cloth in front of them, playing with the keys of their rooms in fingers which shook. There was surprisingly little conversation.

If, at such a moment, the raised voice of the hotel manager could be heard, because somebody had broken a plate in the kitchen, or because of some other trivial accident, I would see these refugees become uneasy, turning their heads to the floor, feeling guilty that they were there, eating somebody else's food. Bosnians are awkward away from home. Now that ethnic cleansing has spread us all over Europe — and the world — we must learn to become travellers and to live abroad. But it is a fact that Bosnians are uncomfortable in other people's houses, however kindly we are treated. We like our own place. I would watch the faces of the older refugees, alone with their sorrow, badly damaged and lost, probably for the rest of their lives. Sometimes, as I watched them, I would find myself beginning to cry. And Željka too.

'Četniks, **** your mothers!' she would mutter under her breath to cheer us both up. But to tell the truth, we would be thinking of our own mothers with our eyes full of tears, wondering if they were waiting for somebody to give them something to eat.

The younger women looked very different, especially if they came from town. Most of them had somebody or other looking after them, always ready with a bag of potatoes, milk, or biscuits for their children. Little managers and bosses at the refugee hotels were always ready to 'help' the younger women. It didn't cost them anything. All they had to do was to sneak into Caritas, pick up the stuff, and later on sneak into the room without being noticed. Of course they were always noticed.

It was all there in our hotel. I didn't blame the refugees, but it was painful to watch. I found such misery hard to take. These were my people after all, and seeing them behave like that changed my views about a lot of things. I came to value honesty more than I had before. Željka had sex in exchange for German marks, but with her own man on her own terms. She never made any secret of it. These women's children could

113

see everything and some were at the age when they were not likely to forget. One day, when they are 20 years old, they will have that harsh memory of being miserable in childhood while they waited for their mother's door to open, and some old 'uncle', speaking in a foreign accent, giving them sweets from his dirty pockets. Sweets from Caritas, which had been sent for them anyway.

Željka and I accepted another woman into our small world. It was Sabina from Stolac with two little boys, Admir and Nihad. The boys were both very naughty and caused her a lot of trouble. Nihad was 3 years old, very small but strong, with healthy red cheeks. He used to climb everywhere, onto walls and up the branches of trees. And then he would jump off and, laughing, try to run away from Sabina who was after him with a little stick. She would say: 'All I ask is that I manage to take this child home with his head on his shoulders.' I don't know what chance she thought she had of returning to Stolac. Nihad was always in danger, and to see him jumping off a wall three times higher than himself made me catch my breath. He was like a little monkey.

We used to drink coffee together at nine o'clock at night, after we had put the children to bed. Every day was the same. Everything lasted too long. We were becoming more depressed and the hotel staff more nervous. All I could think about was home and my home town. Mostar was only a couple of hours away, but I had very little news and I only rarely received a phone call. The idea of going home made the nights long and painful.

The food became so bad that nobody could really eat it. All we got was beans in some kind of sauce or vegetable soup. The manager explained that he didn't have anything more to give us. Without any money at all, it was difficult to make meals for little Zlatko. Instead, Željka and Sabina were cooking every day for all of us. I felt so useless and guilty, trying to do everything for them I could think of. Unconsciously I was trying to avoid the loss of dignity and self-respect which poverty brings, but very often I felt miserable and ashamed.

One time, my husband, big Zlatko, came to stay with us for a while when he had his four days' leave from the front line above Mostar. Four days on the line and four days off was the rule. But almost immediately he became terribly ill with food poisoning, lying on the floor and vomiting until I was desperate to know what to do for him. Someone had distributed some infected food to the soldiers in their dugouts. Later I heard that in those days the Mostar hospital had been full of HVO soldiers brought back from the line with salmonella poisoning.

Another time, I took little Zlatko to see his father up on the frontier between Bosnia and Croatia. We reached Grude by bus, and waited for hours in that hundred per cent Croatian village, very nervous as two Muslims among all those *ustashe* soldiers hanging around outside the bars. They were rough, primitive men, the worst kind of western Hercegovinians, drinking brandy and boasting of the people they had killed, and were going to kill in this war. I saw one terrible man with a beard, wearing a necklace of something dark blue around his neck. When I looked closer I saw that it was made of severed little fingers. The siren was playing for some reason, making everybody nervous. When big Zlatko finally came, we walked up and down feeling lost, not knowing what to say to each other.

At the beginning of September, children of Bosnian Croat nationality started at the local school. They didn't want Muslim children in because it was 'impossible to make up the time-table'. This made me so angry that I decided to see the headmaster. Having been a headmistress myself, I was determined to make him come up with a better excuse than that. He was very polite in his explanation, but when I told him that

115

the policy of his school was inhuman and unfriendly, the smile on his face suddenly disappeared. He didn't have much time for me after that. I managed to say to him at the end of the interview: 'All right, Mister Headmaster, I wish you a successful school year, and enjoy the variety and culture of your supreme nationality.'

'You'll be in trouble,' Željka warned me. But I was in trouble all the time. I wasn't worried about a new 'trouble'.

We went for a walk one evening, and when we came back there was a man carrying a big bag in front of my room. I couldn't recognize him in the darkness, but when I came closer my heart started to beat rapidly, and all my sad thoughts, all my unhappiness, all my soul exploded when my father put his arms around me, whispering, 'My dear little girl.' I hadn't seen him for seven months, and he looked so tired and thin. He was passing through Podgora with his team. He had only five minutes and Željka made coffee immediately. The bag was full of sweets and food which my mother had been collecting for me all that time. There was a cheese pie and a big cake that she had made herself somehow. I had never noticed before that moment that my father had become old. His hair was grey and dusty; his eyes were so tired.

'I had a difficult day,' he said, and shortly afterwards he had to go.

I shared all the food with Željka and Sabina. They tried to comfort me because everything from that bag reminded me of my mother and my family. I felt sorry for my father and I stayed awake all night thinking about his tired eyes. I felt worse than before he came. I was aching for home. And from that moment I longed for my home town more than ever.

The weather changed. There was thunder and lightning every evening and often it was raining. The children had to be kept inside, and the three of us were desperately trying to keep everything tidy. Dark hotel rooms lose the charm they have in the bright summer.

Everything was sad and dispiriting. I felt worse than ever. The room was full of saucepans, spoons, glasses and table cloths we had taken such pride in purloining from the hotel kitchen; the carpet was sodden with water because it was raining so heavily; our beds, which we had tried to keep clean as long as possible, were covered with children eating biscuits. Željka, Sabina and I sat on chairs sunk in gloom, remembering the past.

Željka broke the silence. 'Do you know what our life here is? The Twilight Zone. That's what it is.'

Sabina and I had to laugh. 'But do you know what the Twilight Zone is?'

'Well, I don't know. But it sounds intelligent.'

Željka really didn't know what it was, and that moment in our lives was not intelligent, but the ridiculous remark was funny enough to make us feel better. The rest of the day, thanks to Željka and her Twilight Zone, were spent in laughter, making jokes and drinking coffee.

One night at Podgora the police arrived, looking for deserters. A very young one came knocking at Željka's door.

'Have you got anybody in there?' he muttered, embarrassed.

'Unfortunately, no. But would you like to pop in for a bit?'

'Oh, no! I mean, yes, I would, but I'm on duty, you see . . . that is to say, I . . . '

In the end the kid ran away.

Željka always had her hands full with fellows interested in her. They were all from Podgora, and all trying to impress the most attractive girl in the place. One of them, Miro, was very persistent. He was a ridiculous, fat man, who walked like a peacock. He had a terrible face, completely without teeth in his upper jaw. As he worked in the food aid store, we all called him 'Caritas'.

One warm evening we were all sitting on the wall,

chatting, when Caritas drove up in his clapped-out white Yugo to find Željka, He struggled out from behind the wheel and slammed the door closed with a nonchalant swing of his arm that he must have copied from Harrison Ford or somebody. He was wearing a ridiculous pair of sun-glasses. He told Željka, but loud enough so that we could all hear him, 'I've got a Mercedes in my garage. This is only for every day, easy to park.'

Then Željka jumped off the wall and said in front of everybody: 'OK, Caritas, you bring that Mercedes here and put a hundred German marks on the windscreen. Then we'll talk business . . . .' That kept him quiet for quite a while.

I wanted to go home. I needed the feeling of home, where everything I touched was mine. Where I wouldn't have to feel guilty for eating other people's food or taking advantage of other people's hard work. The hotel staff used to say to us, 'It's a waste of time preparing food for you lot. What do we get to show for it?' It wasn't our fault that they couldn't be serving meals to foreign tourists and earning tips. There weren't any tourists on this coast now. I became very irritable and edgy.

I knew that my family didn't want us back, because Mostar was still dangerous. They hoped that Zlatko and I would spend the winter in Podgora. Now I understand that they were only thinking of our safety, but at the time I became bitter. I sent a stupid message, 'Thanks for missing me so much!'

Then suddenly I had a lovely surprise. My mother arrived to spend a week with me. To my eyes she looked very unhealthy, pale and exhausted. She had now spent more or less half a year living in the basement, dealing with all kinds of troubles, worrying about my father who was out all the time working on unexploded shells, and later on for my brother who worked for the Red Cross. Every day was a struggle to find enough food to make meals for the family. The circumstances she lived in had changed my mother. She looked nervous and, like my father, much older than before.

She wouldn't eat a lot. She didn't seem to want much, except a few cigarettes and a cup of coffee. Željka gave me some money and I bought a lot of fruit for her and some sweets she liked to have with coffee. Every afternoon we would go for a walk, and she really loved the fresh wind from the sea and the sound of the water on the beach. She didn't talk much about the war and what she had been through.

In the middle of the night I could see she wasn't sleeping. She just lay quietly on the bed with her eyes wide open, one arm raised to her forehead. It was very hard to see her like that. I couldn't do or say anything to help her. Words, phrases, like, 'Don't worry, everything will be all right.' wouldn't make any sense or bring any comfort.

After the first morning coffee she would always seem much better, and I would lie down with my head in her lap. She was so warm, and I craved the same physical contact she always gave me as a child when I was frightened or hurt. She was always a constant source of warmth for me. She still is. I know that if she is alive, she never wakes up without thinking of her children.

When my mother left Podgora, and I came back to reality, I felt empty. All I wanted was to go home. The days were much shorter and colder. It often rained. The unheated room was cold and dark. Sabina and Željka had their own problems. Sabina's little boy caught pneumonia. Željka hadn't seen her boy-friend in a long time, and someone told her that he was in trouble. We had lost our patience for dealing with the children, or even with each other. Everybody wanted to go home. We all needed someone to look after us, because it was really a long time since we had been surrounded by our families to share our troubles. One day in November my husband came to visit us in a car he had borrowed from his brother.

'I am coming home with you,' I told him at once. It took just an hour to pack my things. The rest of the day I spent cleaning the room, while Željka and Sabina organized a party. Željka bought chicken and a bottle of brandy. I felt a little sad to be leaving my friends, but they were so happy for me because I was going home. I knew that I wouldn't see them again.

The next morning they were standing around, waiting to say goodbye. I just wanted to go quickly, because I felt guilty about leaving them. I couldn't look at Željka. She was crying. I kissed all the children: little Nihad, who was still recovering from pneumonia, his brother Admir, and little Tina with her sticky cheeks. Then I kissed Željka and Sabina, and they gave me a present, something wrapped beautifully in pink paper.

'Don't open it now. Open it later, after 10 kilometres,' they said. I could see them waving and Željka crying while the car was leaving. My dear, sweet Željka, I thought.

After some time, as the car was climbing into the mountains towards Bosnia, I opened the present. There was a little yellow box inside, with 50 German marks from each of them, and a note.

'For a new life, for a new start. Love from Sabina and Željka.'

I couldn't stop myself crying while Zlatko was chatting so cheerfully with his father. I felt much better when, later on, the mountains opened out and I could see, down in the valley, my dearest town. I am coming back to you, I thought. I felt so good to see it again. Mostar was down there, scarred and wounded by guns, but beautiful.

BAR 21

My mother used to hate going down into the basement when there was shelling. She complained that there was no air and that she was afraid of cockroaches — so ridiculous. My brother always worried about her. Let me tell you how she was cured of that.

Before the war started, a young Serb of about 18 called Nešo used to live with his parents in a house on the left bank. When the Montenegrin *četniks* came down to the left side of town, Nešo's parents were safe enough at home. But his friends were all on the right side, and if he stayed he would have to join the *četniks* himself, so he decided to swim across like many other young people. It was dangerous because the *četniks* on the left side were shooting, so he had to swim the Neretva in the night.

On the right side he stayed with friends, but it was dangerous for a Serb to be seen on the street, so he spent all his time indoors. After two months hiding in basements he came to the flat on Stjepana Radiča with my father, my mother and my brother, Braćo. My brother offered him shelter for a couple of days, and another Serb, about 25 years old, lived nearby.

Across the square someone had opened a little bar on the ground floor of the opposite block, hoping to make a little money. Actually, it was just an empty room with some chairs and some cans of beer and soft drinks. One warm, quiet day, Nešo was sitting inside this bar where he felt safe because people knew him. In fact many people were sitting and standing both inside and outside the door, because it was such a small place and becoming popular, and such a nice day that you could believe it was peacetime again.

And although it was otherwise a quiet day, the Serbs sent just one shell for some reason, a big 155mm one, and that *granata* exploded on the pavement just four metres from the open door, so that all the people inside the bar were killed. Some of the people outside were killed and others were wounded. Altogether twenty-one young people died by the flying pieces of metal and stone from that one shell. Later on the owner, who had not been there, rebuilt the bar and renamed it the '21'. There were always flowers on the place where the *granata* fell.

Nešo had been sitting just inside the bar on a chair and a large piece of *granata* cut through the side of his head. Immediately after the explosion my brother came running down the stairs and across from the apartment to see what had happened, because most of his friends were in that bar. When he saw the massacre he began screaming like everybody else, because girls and boys were lying covered in blood all over that part of the square. Everything was covered with dust and blood and smoke. He saw his friend Nešo inside, still sitting on the chair with half of his head and face missing. He still had a tin of beer in his hand. Then my brother, because he was confused and didn't know what to do, rushed into the bar and tried to give a hug to Nešo. But when he put his arms round his body, he could feel Nešo's foot pushing down against the floor, still alive, trying to stand up, although half of his head was gone. It only lasted a couple of seconds before he died. He had loved that boy like a younger brother; his face looked so young that you wouldn't even have believed he was 18. Nešo hadn't even started shaving.

Bračo ran back over to our basement and we saw him there, crying and hitting his head against the wall. Our neighbour told my mother what Bračo was doing. Then my mother came quietly down the steps and found that my brother had locked himself into our section of the basement, and that he was crying like a child and his head was covered with blood. She went to hold him. Afterwards that picture was always in her mind and she changed completely. She wasn't bothered by such things as cockroaches or lack of air any more; she changed completely and became strong, so that my brother never worried about her again.

Later Bračo told me that was the most difficult day of his life, and that he could never feel a worse pain, whatever happened to him. He felt a physical pain, and it didn't leave him for a long time. I think that this is why he still drinks so much. He often dreams about it, even now.

HYDRO DAM

There are a lot of hydro-electric generating stations on the Neretva river. The war between Serbs, Bosnians and Croats around Mostar was fought for access to hydro-electric power as much as for land.

The first generating barrage above Mostar was simply known as 'Power Station' to the people of the city. It became very important after the Serbs withdrew from Mostar in the early summer and all the modern bridges were blown up. Now the only way a vehicle could cross the Neretva was to drive along the top of the power station dam.

Crossing the dam was a notoriously dangerous thing to do. Almost every day somebody was killed that way. The *četniks* on the mountains could see it very clearly. Up there they had a big mortar gun of a type known as Zis, and they kept it permanently aimed onto the narrow concrete road on top of the barrage. Zis has a particular sound, and it is very accurate. It was set up so well that the shell came down on the road square every time. Every day that Zis killed some poor soul.

My father had to cross the dam most days; sometimes twice. He always assumed that bombs and shells were things which happened to other people, but never to him. He didn't spend too much time worrying about the Zis. If you don't think about it, it won't happen, he reasoned.

One day he went to cross with four people in his lorry. One of them was a very young, very friendly Croat boy. They stopped for a moment before the dam, where the *četniks* couldn't see them. There had been traffic ahead, and they could hear the Zis working every minute or so, firing high on the mountain and biting into the concrete of the dam. They waited for a break, to make a fast run just after a *granata* had burst.

The strategy wasn't particularly successful. In the middle of the dam a *granata* exploded with a tremendous noise in front of the axle and blew out both front tyres. Nobody could hear anything for a couple of minutes, so deafened were they by the shell. Then my father came to his senses and told his passengers to jump out and roll down the grass bank to the ditch at the bottom by the river. When they were all hiding safely at the bottom of the slope, the five of them held a discussion about the situation.

They were all safe enough for the moment, but the lorry on top of the dam was in the most exposed position imaginable. My father said: 'I can't leave the lorry up there, because the *četniks* are going to destroy it. They will keep pounding it until it rolls off the dam. It will be scrap-iron in half an hour. I have to do something. The rest of you go and hide under the dam near the canal.'

The young Croat helped my father begin changing tyres, taking one off each of the double rear wheels and fitting them to the front with three bolts only. They would work for a few seconds and duck down out of the way. A sniper was working on them all the time, and the *Zis* fired again. You could see the *četniks* quite clearly against the horizon without glasses, working their artillery on top of a big hill. And they could clearly see my father and this young Croat going up and down.

They didn't fix the truck properly, but only securely enough to wobble slowly on loose wheels and crawl out of sight along the dam. In a couple of minutes they were safe, and my father could fix the spares on tightly in his own time.

'You know, you are completely crazy,' the Croat boy said.

But my father had a bigger worry.

124

'You can talk,' he said. 'But I have to go back. That's my big problem.'

There was no other way. After running his errand, whatever it was, he had to come back that way. He knew that the dam and the Zis were waiting.

IVICA

A young Croat fellow called Ivica, aged about 25, worked in the little shop at the bottom of 16A Matije Gupča. He was not a Croat like those from Listisča or Čitluk, but a Mostar boy and very friendly to everybody. He sold food there, working for the owner who was a Muslim. Can you imagine that? Only a good Croat can do that. You didn't have any problems if you were short of money and you needed something if Ivica was in the shop. He would say, 'OK, don't worry, I'll write it down,' to make you feel better, but you could see he wasn't writing, because people didn't have money as the war went on.

I spent a lot of time sitting on the steps in front of the block with Ivica by that shop, because it was dangerous to go further and all you could do anyway was sit. We had a game of tavla there about a week before the fighting broke out between the Brigade and the HVO, and I know that he was a better player than I was, but he let me win. He told me that he had always wanted to go to Australia, and I asked why. He said that he liked the idea of all those open spaces and he wanted to work at catching kangaroos — to shake those silly animals up a bit. I had to laugh.

About that time I noticed he became rather nervous. I asked him, 'Please tell me if everything is going to be all right? What do you think?'

He answered, 'It's not going to be all right. I am afraid.' He had the opportunity to know; maybe somebody in the HVO had talked to him. Muslims were always asking such questions because we were desperate to hear some good news.

Two days after the fighting started in the city, we were on the landing when he suddenly came out of the lift. He was dressed in the uniform of the HVO, with badges, everything, and with two guns, a Kalashnikov assault rifle and a pistol. All the people from that building, except my father-in-law, were hiding in the one place. When we saw his familiar face we all jumped up with relief from the stairs and the floor — and then we saw that he was crying. He really burst into tears when he saw us. He threw the guns on the floor and then tore his badge off and threw that on the floor, too, then sat down with his face in his hands, crying all the time. He sobbed, 'Please, friends, hide all the Muslims somewhere. Help neighbours. If there is a God, He's not going to forgive us.'

He told us that they had collected him two days before and given him the guns and the badge — ' . . . and I have just come back from Drežnica, and we killed them all there, women and children, too.' He was crying all the time, very bitterly, and saying constantly, 'Please hide the Muslims, please hide the Muslims.'

Later on I was very ashamed of myself because I noticed that he needed a handkerchief. I didn't have one, and I can't stand to look at someone's nose running, so I didn't look at him directly. I should have looked my friend in the face, sticky nose or not.

Later, Ivica had to go. He collected the guns from the floor and a Muslim lady gave him the HVO badge back. The lady said, 'You mustn't go outside without this, dear; you know that, don't you?' And he put the badge in his pocket and disappeared in the lift. We never saw him again.

He is probably dead now. He was too weak for a soldier. Too gentle. Someone will have killed him. Muslims or Croats. He wasn't good for them. Neither for one side nor the other. That's the worst tragedy, the most unforgivable crime in all of this. The best people — they just have to die.

JOZO AND OSMAN

One day, when the fighting was at its worst, I was sitting with friends on the landing of the sixth floor. It wasn't safe to be in our flat on the first floor. It faced towards the Boulevard and the monastery, so it was too exposed and too low. We could hear the sound of a lot of heavy artillery fire at that moment. Snipers were working from the windows of the higher flats facing towards the line, and every thirty seconds or so we could hear the thump of the mortar on our roof. While we waited, drinking coffee and smoking and shivering, two soldiers came up the stairs. You could always recognize the noise soldiers made on the stairs. Their boots were so heavy, and the guns on their shoulders and the grenades and spare magazines hanging from their webbing knocked against the walls and the metal railing. Everybody went quiet. When the heads became visible above the edge of the stairwell, we could just see the word *Juka* printed on their caps.

We were almost frightened to death, but the soldiers just said, 'Good day,' and went politely and quietly into Zijada's flat. After a while Zijada came out and announced, 'They are going to look after us. Juka sent them because of Mirsada.'

Zijada's sister Mirsada was a friend of Juka, and the owner of the *Little Paris* restaurant. Mirsada had asked Juka for guards because their mother was bed-ridden in the flat and she didn't want anyone from the HVO to bother them. That particular Muslim family was well cared for, whatever happened to anybody else. Mirsada tried to keep in with everybody. Her *Little Paris* restaurant had fed all Juka's soldiers through the war, and in return the restaurant got the pick of whatever supplies of food and whisky were available. They never drank anything but Scotch at the *Little Paris*.

Mirsada was a big handsome woman of about 40, very powerful in her connections and character, married to a quite remarkably rich and stupid man. Juka was small and ugly, with the silly face of a teenager never grown up, always trying to look dangerous. Of course he *was* dangerous. But he and Mirsada were never a pair. She kept plenty of little tarts around the *Little Paris* for Juka and his soldiers, or for anyone else who turned up with the cash to pay for one of the comfortable rooms upstairs. The *Little Paris*, you must understand, was something more than just a restaurant.

Mirsada reserved herself for the big bosses. Safet was one for sure. She did her best to keep in with every-body, HVO and the Armija. If General Mladić had arrived with an army of *četniks*, she would probably have been pouring whisky for him. All she cared about was money and saving her restaurant, which before the war had been the largest and most expensive in Mostar. I could only afford to eat there once. Mirsada used to sing there herself with a small band, under the nickname *Kalimera*, as if she were a Greek.

Juka's two soldiers came out of the flat and stood guarding the door, very bored and smelling very badly. Maybe they were missing the baths at the *Little Paris*. It was hot and the landing was crowded. I was sitting on the door, talking, but after a while I realized that they were looking at me. They had heard little Zlatko calling me 'Mama', and some of the neighbours had used my name.

I was already exposed in a dangerous position, so I decided to take a chance. I started a conversation to see what sort of people they were.

'What do you think? Will this fighting ever stop?'

I spoke in a spontaneous, artless way, without appearing to mean anything in particular. It was always important to see what people were thinking before you revealed your own thoughts. Especially when those people had two guns each and a big knife hanging from their belt.

The younger soldier, who was only about 17, said, 'I don't know. My brother is in the Bosnian Army in Sarajevo, and look where I am.' He was a Muslim, caught up with Juka fighting for the HVO in Mostar. His name was Osman.

The other man, who looked about 40 and was definitely the smellier of the two, said, 'Nobody is asking us about anything. I never imagined I would end up like this, guarding an old lady of about a hundred in bed. I feel like a complete idiot.' Jozo was a Croat from central Bosnia.

Then I realized that they weren't dangerous, apart from the smell. Their guns and their knives didn't bother me. So I started chatting to them. The boy was paying me compliments, telling me that I was too young to have a son of Zlatko's age. We were all very cheerful there on the landing, making jokes and laughing. They gave me a cigarette and offered me one of their cans of beer, which I refused. I felt safer than before, despite all the noise outside. Outside was like hell.

At one point I asked Jozo: 'What do you think? Will the left side surrender?'

He gave me a most incredible answer, something completely unexpected. He said: 'What is the left side?'

He wasn't from Mostar and didn't have a clue which army held which side of the city. He only knew that Croats and Muslims were fighting.

'The left side belongs to Muslims,' I told him.

'Aha, aha,' he said, in the way that Croats do when they are thinking. 'Well, personally speaking, if I was on the left side, I wouldn't surrender.'

I started to like Jozo a lot, because he had such a healthy attitude about fighting and not surrendering. He wasn't like all the other neighbours on the landing, Croats and Muslims, too, who only wanted the left side to surrender as quickly as possible so that all this suffering could be over. But was he genuine? He knew that I was a Muslim. Maybe it was a provocation to draw a reaction from me. We had already had some nasty little games of that kind. At the beginning of the week a group of HVO soldiers had made their way into Muslim flats in the block on the other side of Matija Gupča, wearing Armija shoulder badges on their uniforms. As they had hoped, the Muslims there had almost embraced them with relief: 'Thank God you are here, you have saved our lives,' and so on. After which they had stripped the flats and beaten everybody up, talking about it afterwards as though it was something very funny. And the Armija had played some games of their own, several times sending soldiers dressed in HVO uniforms through the sewers under the Boulevard, to emerge on the banks of the Radabolja stream and mount ambushes behind our flats. So everybody was frightened and cautious. In reply to Jozo I said simply: 'Well, I think they should', just to defend myself in case he was intelligent. But he wasn't.

We spent two days talking on that landing, and they were very generous with their cigarettes. Other HVO soldiers were going up and down with ammunition, but nobody bothered us with Juka's men there. We felt safe.

On the third morning they were not in their usual place. Zijada told me that Juka had needed them and they had to go. She didn't know if they would be back. Maybe yes, maybe no. There was particularly heavy shelling going on outside that day and we could also hear the sound of gas bottles exploding in burning flats. Even Mirsada's mother was out of the flat, lying in bed on the landing. We were afraid of shrapnel coming through the windows.

That was the day of the great explosion at Tito Bridge. Afterwards we heard that the HVO had packed a lorry with explosives and rolled it down the slope towards Šantic Street and the bridge, hoping to destroy it. I was on an empty landing at the time. Suddenly I felt the floor shake as if there was an earthquake and I was unable to walk. In front of me were two Muslim flats, stripped and empty, the doors standing open. The terrible sound of the explosion came and suddenly the shuttered aluminium window of one flat, complete with its frame, came flying right across the landing, driven in by the blast.

Mišo 'Gvardijan' came up the stairs to the landing and shouted: 'Nerma! Senada! Get out of here and do something useful. White ribbon on your left shoulder, red ribbon on your right.' Mišo was a Croat whom the HVO had put in charge of two blocks of flats. He used to be a friend of my brother-in-law, Dragan. Before the war they gambled together every night. Now he wanted us to work in his office on the ground floor of the next block.

We put on our ribbons. The white was to show that we were Muslim; the red that we were working for the HVO that day. I tied my red ribbon round my head like Rambo. Senada was shaking with fear. She was about 40 and divorced, and was hiding a son of military age in her flat. Everybody knew that he was there. Then we had to run across to the HVO office, where we found two Croatian girls, Mariana and Zravka, and a lot of soldiers hanging around. They made me type, but Senada just sat shivering, so after half an hour they told her to go. The documents I had to type were orders allocating Muslim flats in Mostar to HVO soldiers from Lištica and Medugorje.

Mišo came and sat at the only proper desk, his boots on the table. He was feeling important for the first time in his life. It was his first taste of power. He looked like a real bastard, lounging there, his boots among all the guns laid down on the desk. He was supposed to be in charge of 'security' for the two blocks, to make sure everyone was safe and nothing got stolen.

One of the soldiers came in with a big suitcase full of whisky and another had found a box of fresh oranges. I can't think how they managed to find such stuff in Mostar. They got busy pouring whisky and squeezing the oranges for juice, making a complete mess everywhere. I had finished all the typing by then, so Mišo told me to go back to my flat and make coffee and bring it to them.

'Run quickly and keep your head low,' he told me.

I stood by the entrance, not knowing what to do. Sniper's bullets were cracking past outside and shells were coming in.

'Go on,' said Mišo. 'You'll be OK. I'll cover you.'

I was thinking that he had seen too many western films. What the hell did he mean by that? What exactly does 'I'll cover you' mean, anyway? I was almost laughing and crying at the same time as I ran across.

In the flat I made a big *ibrik* full of coffee, put it on a tray with sugar and milk and all the cups I could find, and came down to the entrance. My hands were shaking by now and everything was moving on the tray. Some mortar shells were exploding outside, so close that I couldn't tell whether they were incoming or outgoing, or just badly aimed. I stood shaking for a moment against the wall in the shelter of the first balcony, telling myself that I would go as soon as there was a quiet moment. I only had to run 10 metres, but I couldn't make myself move. I could hear the sound of sniper's bullets in the air close by. Then Mišo saw me from the door of the office. He was quite safe where he was standing, protected by a wall of sand bags.

'Come on,' he shouted. 'Don't be silly. It's our people shooting.'

Our people, his people, my people. I guessed that one bullet would feel much like another. But I had to run with the tray, and I reached the door of the office. Inside, I served coffee to everybody, my hands trembling so badly that I spilled it twice.

'Relax,' said Mariana, stretching out her legs.

'Tomorrow at the same time,' said Mišo. Then he went to the fridge and gave me a jar of chocolate spread for my son.

That was a terrible day and the shelling never stopped. Everybody felt lost and terrified. We went to bed, but we couldn't sleep for the sound of the drunken shouting outside which went on all through the night.

'Muslims! We're going to drink your blood. Muslims! Do you hear?'

In the early hours we heard the sound of a Muslim woman screaming from one of the blocks on the far side of Matija Gupča. They say that she was raped by more than thirty soldiers. I began shivering so badly that nothing could make me warmer. I remembered all the stories of Jasenovac concentration camp from the Second World War, how the ustaša guards there drank the blood of Serbs. So I lost control. I couldn't deal with myself or the situation any more.

But in the morning Zijada called me up to her flat, and there were Jozo and Osman. They just came to say hello and check on Mirsada's mother, but seeing them standing there I felt safe again. I gave them both a hug and didn't mind them smelling at all. They gave me chocolate and two whole packets of cigarettes. Jozo said, 'Don't worry. It will be all right. Things will calm down. We'll come again tomorrow and see that you are OK.'

I asked, 'Is it possible that someone could come to my door and kill my son, and I can't do anything about it? Please tell me it can't happen.'

I was crazy that morning. Of course I knew that it couldn't happen. But I wanted somebody to say something to reassure me.

Jozo said: 'Of course not. Don't worry. Things like that only happen in the villages. Relax. We'll come back tomorrow.'

The next day the meeting about a ceasefire in Mostar was held at Medugorje, and the city was a little quieter. Zlatko and I went to his brother Dragan's flat to see if he was safe. When we got back to Matija Gupča 16A I saw Oliver's blue Land Rover standing by the steps.

LETTER FROM UNCLE DŽEVO
left bank, 18 October

My dear family,

I received a letter from Zlatko, which made me so upset. But happy to find some news of you all. I was crying like a child, and at one point I gave it to little Adla to read to me. You can imagine how it is to receive a letter from your nearest relatives after five months.

Firstly, we are all alive. We live under very difficult conditions, and so I cannot say that we are also healthy. First hunger and now starvation. All the time we live in the basement without electricity, water, toilets and everything you need for ordinary life. Places intended for dogs and cats and rats and spiders are now for people to live in. Our old people, especially Semiya, look like the photographs we used to see of Dachau and Auschwitz. Semiya can't see anything any more, and she can't hear. Her weight is 38kg. Me, from 84kg to 65kg now; Belka, from 80kg to 60kg, and so on.

About the children: Adla is the weakest one. She was always skinny, you remember.

Until a couple of days ago we had a public kitchen, and one daily meal for everybody, though without bread. But now we haven't even got that. There is no food in store to prepare any more meals. They gave us 1kg of flour, 0.2kg of oil, and a tin of fish yesterday. Who knows when they are going to repeat this? The blockade of the left bank of the Neretva is so perfect that not even a bird can carry anything across to prevent us starving on this side. It's not a question of money at the moment, because there is nothing to buy.

About safety outside: You know that we have to go out on the street for water form the tanker (Neretva water treated with chlorine), or to find some food, or maybe to find a couple of pieces of wood to cook something in the basement. We make a fire between two stones, like in Žepa or Srbreniča. Shells are falling everywhere in the town, constantly, like rain. There is no weapon they are not using to shell us. Ten to twelve killed or wounded is the average every day.

About destruction on this side: Vukovar cannot be compared to this at all. Your flat has been completely destroyed. Three shells came into Semiya's flat. There is no roof there at all. Nowadays, with shelling and snipers, we mend our roofs at night, by the light of the moon. Safer's house has been completely destroyed by one shell from a tank and three from a mortar gun. We are trying to save what we can of the contents.

My dearest family, I could write for a long time about what has been happening here over these five months, and I would need a lot of paper for that. But this is all for now. We are alive. We are having a very difficult time. But we are going to survive.

Take care. Lots of love to everybody on the right side.

DŽEVO.

CHECKPOINTS

Checkpoint jokes circulated all the time in Hercegovina, and most of them involved Croats, who do have a sense of humour. Some of the ustaša villages, particularly Gruda, developed the habit of being difficult and obstructive at checkpoints to an art form. But in the jokes the tactics usually rebound on the perpetrator.

For instance, there was the case of the man, a western Hercegovinian Croat and a ustaša to boot, who drove up to a checkpoint near Gruda and presented a Hercog-Bosnia identity card provided by the HVO, with a photograph of the man's bearded face, and complete with the Croatian chequered shield and all necessary signatures and stamps. This should have presented no problem, particularly as the man came from the next village and was known to the sentry.

But the sun was hot, and the sentry was feeling bloody-minded, as sentries on checkpoints often do.

'How come this photograph doesn't look like you?' he asked the driver.

'But it does look like me. Of course it's me. It's just that I shaved my beard last month. My wife didn't like it.'

'Look here,' said the sentry. 'That just isn't good enough. You can't go wandering about with a photograph that doesn't look like you. It's wartime, after all. Our job is hard enough as it is.'

'So can't I pass?'

'No, you can't.'

'Fair enough,' said the driver. And he reversed his car back a few metres from the barricade and stopped the engine, wound the driver's window right down, and subsided into the seat with his feet sticking out of the window.

For about ten minutes there was no sound but the singing of birds around the checkpoint. The sentry paced up and down in the hot sun, sweating, and occasionally glancing at the parked car and the motionless feet. At last he could stand it no longer. He marched over to the window and demanded: 'So why are you hanging around?'

The driver opened his eyes reluctantly.

'Oh, don't mind me, please. You just carry on with your duties and I'll keep growing my beard again. I mean, everything takes time. We must be patient!'

Another example involved the HVO soldier who drove his car up to another such checkpoint somewhere in Hercegovina, and showed his papers.

'Yellow card?' demanded the sentry.

'What?'

'Yellow card. I have orders to check them.'

'What yellow card? I never had one. Who issues them?'

'How do I know? I just know you have to have one.'

'Well, what does this yellow card look like, then?

Show it to me.'

'I haven't got one.'

'Why not?'

'I don't need one. But you need one.'

As before, the soldier reversed his car a few yards, but in this case he swung it across to block the road and got out with his rifle. Almost at once another car came up the road, and the soldier with the rifle waved it down and began to talk to the driver. The sentry at the checkpoint walked down to see what was going on.

'What do you think you're doing?'

'Orange cards.'

'What?'

'I'm asking for orange cards.'

'You can't do that.'

'Why not? You've got a gun; I've got a gun. That's your checkpoint; this is my checkpoint. You carry on with your yellow cards. Me, I'm asking for orange cards. Nobody gets past my checkpoint without an orange card!'

EMINA

Last night, when I was coming
Back from the warm baths,
I was passing the gardens of the old Imam,
And at that moment, in the garden,
In the shade of a jasmine,
With a water jar in her hands,
There was Emina.

And I swear to God I said *Selam* to her,
But she would not listen, beautiful Emina.
She just looked at me for a moment
With a frown on her face.
She never cared that I was amazed by her beauty,
She drew her water from the well,
And walked away through the garden.

Then I felt the wind blowing from the Neretva,
And I saw the wind unbraiding her hair,
Making her breasts move,
And making her *shalvar* trousers shimmer.

Now the old poet has died,
And Emina is dead,
And the jasmine garden is deserted.

ALEKSA ŠANTIĆ
Nineteenth century (Serb) poet from Mostar.

JOSIP MARIĆ (GENIUS)

Josip was about the same age as little Zlatko, just a bit taller, with bright blue eyes and brown hair. He used to wear a white T-shirt, usually not too clean, on which he had written himself with a magic marker pen: *Josip Marić (genius)*. I can see him now in that T-shirt, sitting all alone on the flat roof of the concrete garages below our block, holding an umbrella over his head to keep of the spring rain, waiting for Zlatko to finish his breakfast and come down to join him. He always looked so small and innocent like that, waiting for Zlatko and waiting for the sun. He was quick and bright, full of spirit and fun, as you might expect from one who had decided to label himself genius.

Josip was a Croatian boy, whose family had come to Mostar from Grude. I liked him the best of all Zlatko's friends, partly because whenever I had a gang of little boys around my feet, Josip was always well behaved and only needed to be told anything once. His parents were pretty tough with him, probably because he was one of four children. For that reason, Josip never had as many sweets and toys as an only child like Zlatko. I advised little Zlatko to share everything with Josip, his best friend, because he had no sister or brother. I remembered my own childhood in which I had to settle for half of everything because the other half belonged to my brother. While I was just a child it took me a long time to understand that my brother needed his share. Even more difficult than that, my brother needed to learn to share with me. I had to grow up to see that. And finally I did, though it took some time.

Josip spent a lot of time with us, and I came to realize that nobody was ever looking for him, even late in the evening when children couldn't be seen playing outside any more. His parents were very religious and believed that Almighty God looks after little children, and that is more than enough. Zlatko enjoyed having Josip around, and especially when he stayed overnight with us, which was quite often. I liked the idea myself. There was never any misunderstanding or rivalry between these two boys. They were two best mates, closer than brothers.

I used to make them cakes and ice-cream in the summer time, and then I would call down from my balcony to where they were playing on top of the garage roofs, 'Zlatko! Josip! Ice-cream is ready!'

They loved to be called like that. In a moment they would be racing up the stairway to see who would be first. It was usually Josip of course. His reactions were so quick that he would jump up in an instant and start to run. Zlatko was a little overweight, which slowed him down in the race for ice-cream.

The two boys had some pets. Personally I have never much liked animals, except in photographs or when they are very young. But I never wanted Zlatko to have the same prejudices, so I decided to help him develop genuine feelings towards some pets of his own. So we had birds, a rabbit, and for one crazy period, even a little dog. Zlatko was delighted with the idea and looked after all these small creatures with Josip. I used to enjoy hearing them talking about their rabbit, whose name was Smrdo — Smelly.

'Please, Smelly, stop pooing, or we'll put you in the washing machine!'

The roof of the big block of garages was their

favourite place. On a warm afternoon you could look down from the balcony and see at least fifty children of their age on that flat roof, sitting, playing cards, or just standing around discussing the latest cartoon, 'Tall Man with his Wonderful Cat'. What did worry me was to see the children running on the top, playing tag. It really was dangerous and of course they weren't careful. I had my own theory about who looks after little children. Someone told me, 'You can't forbid children to climb. Just relax.' Of course I couldn't relax, but I couldn't stop them climbing either. Fortunately, we never had an accident. Josip loved the garages more than any of them. He was up there first in the morning and last to leave at night.

Little Zlatko and Josip played all through those beautiful days in Mostar when the only problem for children was bedtime. Everything in their life was wonderful, challenging and exciting, as it should be for children. In summer they would be outside from morning to dusk, only coming back for a quick bite. On hot afternoons we would take them to Buna, a nice little village south of Mostar by the river. The bathing pool there would be full of children swimming and playing. When there was a little money around we would go for a weekend or even a week by the seaside, and Josip was always with us. My country was such a good place for children to play then: safe and warm. People never minded ball games or the noise they made, or told them to keep off the grass. All our children were always outside, and you could be sure that they were all making a noise. Someone once asked my neighbour, watching the children playing in the water at Buna, 'How many of those are yours?'

'Seven,' he replied.

'I haven't got any children yet,' the other remarked.

'Would you like me to catch you one in a net?' he laughed.

War came suddenly among us, covering our valley

like a black cloud from across the mountains. Everybody was afraid, but the more children people had, the more afraid they were. What was to be done with them? Where were they to be hidden? How were they to be fed? When I ran away from Mostar many others did the same, and we didn't have time to tell each other where we were running to. For a long time I had no news of Josip and his family. In Serbia, and later in Podgora, little Zlatko talked about Josip all the time. We both missed him. I only hoped that they were safe with their relatives in Grude.

When we returned to Mostar I decided one day to visit my flat and the old neighbourhood. The garages were deserted, and the playground too. I couldn't see or hear any children at all. It seemed so strange for the place to be so quiet. All the blocks of flats were damaged and there were hardly any glass windows left. The people I met were strange to me, obviously not from Mostar. They looked sad and lost, these refugees, especially the elderly. The shutters were pulled down over the windows of Josip's flat. The family must be in Grude, I thought to myself.

Then I saw a familiar face. It was Zijada, one of my old neighbours, on her way home wheeling a plastic barrel of water on a trolley. After a short conversation I asked if she knew what had happened to the Marić family. I almost wished that I hadn't asked at all.

'Josip — they lost Josip,' she said, her eyes filling with tears. She told me what had happened in a couple of minutes, and then walked on to her flat with a handkerchief held over her nose. The wheels of her trolley were groaning and squeaking as she dragged it along.

I wanted to scream 'Where is the one who looks after little boys? Where is he now?' I still haven't had the courage to tell Zlatko the whole truth.

Josip Marić had been sitting alone on the garage roof, just like in the old days when he waited for little Zlatko to finish his breakfast or for me to make ice-cream. How could he have known that his sudden death was coming to him out of the bright sky which before had brought him only sun or gentle spring rain on his umbrella? Far away in the mountains by Nevesinje, they had loaded the shining cylinder marked with black cyrillic characters into the breech, pulled a cord and sent the contents on their long journey through the atmosphere. The shell had hit the wall of the block opposite and a piece of shrapnel found Josip Marić just as he jumped up to run. This time he wasn't quick enough and, anyway, there was no ice-cream for him.

ONCE IN MOSTAR

The summers in Mostar were always the same. Every year there were long, very hot periods without any rain or breeze. The grass was green until May or June, but then it would change colour to yellow. Nobody liked to walk on the hot streets after midday, but sometimes you could see a bus with an exhausted driver, a wet handkerchief wrapped around his head.

The brave thing for children to do at that time of day was to walk from the Music School across Tito Bridge to Hit shopping centre. That was a very long street, with no shade at all in the summer. If you looked down from the bridge on a day like that, you saw hundreds of fig trees hanging from both banks of the river and powerful green water running south, making curves to the left and to the right, as if the Neretva was indecisive despite its speed and strength, before it pushed down to the Old Bridge and beyond.

I remember once walking that street, among the houses of the city, with the tickling smell of paprikas and fried fish coming through the opened windows, and *salša*, which is home-made bread and tomatoes chopped and stirred in oil with garlic and peppers. People's washing hung from small balconies. An elderly couple sat at their window, nervous and confused, trying to survive the long hot day, irritated by everything and everyone, although after seven in the evening they would even be prepared to talk to each other. There was a smell of coffee from somewhere and loud Bosnian folk music playing on the radio. A dark-skinned figure sat reading a newspaper outside the little ice-cream shop which stayed open until late. Somebody's blue baby Fiat was being repaired at the garage, and from inside the dark workshop came the smell of good Hercegovinian tobacco and the sound of arguing voices.

A boy dressed only in swimming trunks was riding his bike aimlessly around the bus station. Wasn't he hot? No, he was too young to be hot. Or cold. Some people were waiting for a bus, which was terribly late. In the shade of a block of flats a couple were leaning against a wall, kissing. A bunch of kids began teasing them; the fellow shouted and they ran away laughing.

By now there was a small crowd waiting. People had had enough. They were angry, swearing at the absent driver. The bus was more than an hour late. 'What does he think we are, cattle?'

A couple of tourists approached the bus station, very elderly, over 80, shaking as they walked slowly, hand in hand.

'Is this the final trip, young chap?' shouted some wag in the crowd, teasing them for their age. Everybody laughed and the old foreign couple laughed too. What friendly people here, they probably thought.

Finally the bus arrived, and nobody was cross with the driver any more.

'Better late than never,' somebody dared to say. But the bus driver was very hot and annoyed himself. Attack is always the best line of defence.

'I am paid so badly that you had better be grateful that I am here at all,' he retorted.

Emptiness at the bus station. Only the kid riding his bike restlessly in circles and dustbins overflowing with rubbish. A soldier in uniform, sitting alone on the bench. I noticed that he was reading a dirty magazine. And when he realized that a young girl was watching him, he slid an ordinary newspaper over it, *Free Dalmatia* or something, and pretended to read that.

I wish that I could see such a soldier at our bus station again. He was so ashamed of his sex magazine. It wasn't such a big deal. His friends in Mostar are so different now. So shamelessly they carry their obscene guns in their dirty hands. And nothing on their conscience. Nothing at all.

Suddenly, in my pain, I want to go home. I want my cup of coffee and my own bathroom. I want that precious town of Mostar, my home town, that diamond, that 'city of light' as Ivo Andrić once called it, all around me again. I remember that wonderful feeling of having my town around me. But I know that I have lost it for ever.

MY FATHER'S WAR

When the war first started with the Serbs, I was still at home with my family in the basement. At that point the shelling was between the HVO and the *četniks* from hill to hill. Nobody touched Mostar in the beginning.

The HVO held only a short stretch of the mountains around the city, perhaps two kilometres long. The rest of the high ground was all occupied by the *četniks*, who wanted to push the HVO back so that they could close a complete ring around Mostar. If ever they did that, nobody would be able to get in or out. We all knew that. The Posusje/Listisca road was still open, but the hills were covered with *četniks*.

The Croats were very determined to defend their single hill on the north-west, and deny the little military road which they had built two months before to the Serbs. The HVO had known what was coming and had taken the best possible action. We in Mostar had been afraid of war, but without any idea of the danger our city was really in.

The *četniks* shelled that little hill until it was covered all over with holes. Later, when the Serbs had retreated a few kilometres, people used to make a trip from Mostar just to look at the way their howitzers had eaten away at that hill. We could all hear the explosions, but my father pretended that he wasn't afraid because I was so terribly worried and frightened. I couldn't function at all, but just sat in the basement crying. It was the first time in my life I had heard the sound of shells and rockets.

My father said: 'It's as if they have an arrangement. They're just saying hello from hill to hill.'

He was trying to cheer me up. Not long afterwards I escaped from the city and went to Serbia.

My father always parked his lorry in front of the flat at Stjepana Radica, because it was a long way to walk to the depot on the left bank. When the *četniks* came down from the mountains and occupied the left side, his lorry was safe in the new part of the city. He felt that he ought to use it in some way for Mostar, so he drove it to the office of the Bosnian Croat army, HVO, and offered his services: 'I've still got my truck. But the company's depot on the left side is occupied by *četniks*. Can I do something with it to help?'

So the HVO formed a little group of workers to remove unexploded shells safely. These defective *granatas* usually buried themselves deep in the ground, but it would have been very dangerous to leave them there. A couple of specialists had been trained in the work, and at first my father was just a driver. But later on all the members of the group learned how to handle explosives. They were taught the safest way to dig the earth away around the *granata* to make it approachable. How to make it safe. How to put it on the lorry and take it away.

It was a good way to find food. My family expected

the war to end some day, but we were all frightened of being hungry. It had struck my father that the shortage of food was likely to continue for some time after the war, so he decided to collect as much as possible for the entire family. He wanted to make a reserve for two households. He collected tins and everything he could possibly find. He was able to ask for food everywhere, because his HVO group was moving around so much behind the front. Most of it came from church organizations. Croatian churches were always asking for defused examples of Serbian shells to exhibit, presumably as propaganda. The churches at Listisca and Citluk must have been full of them. In return, they were very happy to trade a case of tinned beef or a bag of rice. He collected so much that he was able to give some to all the neighbours.

My father worked most of that year with his little explosives group. He was much happier outside, because he couldn't bear to stay in the basement for more than ten minutes, even during curfew. Everybody from the block used to sleep in the basement except him. He would be sleeping upstairs in the flat, pretending that the shelling and shooting outside didn't frighten him. He was always in the flat. My mother told me that in all the time I was away, during all those bombardments, he only came down to the basement twice, and never for more than ten minutes. He couldn't take it down there. He was too irritated by people's depression and crying and screaming.

One night in early June 1992, before the _četniks_ retreated from the left bank, the HVO wanted him to drive for them. It was about ten o'clock in the evening. Outside it was hell. My father's group collected him, and they explained that they would be busy that night.

'We are going to protect the Old Bridge, before the _četniks_ destroy it.'

The _četniks_ were all along the left bank of the river then, right at the end of the bridge.

So my father and his group had to go first to the

prison with the lorry, to collect about twenty četnik prisoners who were going to carry out the work on the bridge. That is the system, you know, in this war. Of course it breaks the Geneva convention. It was very dangerous to go anywhere near the bridge, because it is so close to the left bank. They would not stop shelling and sniping, not for one moment. The shellings were terrible when the četniks were on the left side, never stopping for a clear minute. The Serbs have so much ammunition that they never worry about how much they use. Bosnia will be covered with Vukovars by the time they finish.

They collected twenty četniks from the prison, and then they needed boards, scaffolding and boiler plating from different places in the city. There was a battle raging all the time. Finally my father had to manoeuvre the big loaded lorry down that narrow street without lights, through the old bazaar until he brought them within a few metres of the end of the bridge. Then they shouted across with a megaphone to the Serbs on the far bank.

'The people on the bridge are yours. So if you want to shoot, we are not bothered at all. If you decide to shoot at the bridge, you are killing your own people.'

The četniks stopped firing when their prisoners were on the bridge. They shelled all other parts of Mostar for the rest of that night, but not the Old Bridge. Everything was done in the dark. The steel scaffolding was bolted to the parapet, and wooden boards and steel plates were fixed to make a protecting roof over the single arch of the bridge. Everything was done by hand, in the dark, and in a single night. Nobody was hurt.

In the morning my father had to take the prisoners back to gaol and then drive the members of his group to their homes in various parts of the city. He came home very early. The family were still in the basement, very frightened, nobody moving. Nobody expected him

147

back alive, because it had been so bad outside that night.

But someone had given my father a bottle of home-made black wine and he was cheerful. He just sat down in the corner and stretched his legs, pulled the cork and drank a big mouthful of wine and winked at them.

THE TRIAL OF THE MAN OF CA

It happened that on a certain day a man of the Ca tribe was walking on a long and lonely road. He saw, coming towards him, a man with a woman carrying a baby. As they drew closer the man of Ca saw that the other man was of the fierce Ke tribe and that he carried in his hand a long knife. As they drew level and began to pass each other the man of Ca drew out an even longer knife which he had concealed and fell upon the man of Ke and cut and stabbed him to death. He also stabbed to death the screaming woman. After wiping his knife on grass by the roadside he walked on.

In due course the authorities, having made enquiries of the people who lived at either end of the road, arrested the man of Ca and he was brought to trial. He admitted the killing but denied that it was murder.

'For,' he said, 'everyone knows that the Ke are a fierce and warlike tribe, full of hate for others. This man was very strong and in the prime of his life. It is likely that he had killed many people and that he would have killed many more in the numberless wars caused by the Ke. Far from condemning me for this act the peoples of the civilized tribes should honour me for having saved them from much evil.'

There were loud cheers at this, for many people of the Ca were in court and none had any love for the Ke. But the judge silenced them and said to the accused.

'It was not only the man whom you killed; the woman also you stabbed to death and the baby, left uncared for, succumbed to thirst and the heat of the sun before being found. You surely cannot have seen evil in the child?'

The man of Ca replied, 'The death of the woman I regret but it was unavoidable because she stood beside the man and would have identified me. As for the baby, I must admit I do not feel concerned. It is true that, while a baby, he was innocent but he would have grown to manhood with the Ke. They would have taught him all their warlike ways and, in the course of time, our own children would have suffered at his hands. I still think I am due more praise than blame.'

More cheers followed, but not as many as before. The Judge said, 'If it were to be considered right to kill any man who might do harm then none possessing limbs could be left alive. You have done great wrong which will not stop at the death of the woman and child. Until now the people of Ca have been renowned for their love of peace and the high value they place on civilisation. From thenceforward and by the generations to come none will trust a man of Ca when he speaks of peace. It may be that you have condemned us all.'

W. M. REYNOLDS

LAMENTATION –
for all Bosnians against Nationalism

I cannot sing, no, I'm afraid I cannot sing about this. There is a knot of anger and frustration blocking my chest and this embolism prevents the proper flow in the channels of thought from becoming proper words.

Similarly someone pushed to helpless silence glares, bares teeth like an animal cornered, and bashes with a gun. At times, snapping off the radio in dread of disgust, I have touched on a smouldering silence. I posture slipping out the back door, walking-boots and a dark coat with deep pockets: 'Gone to join the gun-runners.'

For, those who didn't want to fight have been forced to fight; those who wanted to live, not in a nation but in a place — planting, harvesting, merchandising, factory shift, building, chaffering, inviting people to weddings, visiting neighbours, with the usual greeds loves losses imagination stupidity tolerance hopes and failures, person to person, trade to trade — their place their domus their society their country — have been forced into a *laager*, turned back into a tribe, taught to pull down the shutters and bare the teeth and growl if a stranger should pause at their shop, where formerly he would be asked in to take a beaker of tea while he looked at the wares. They have been trained and degraded into pack dogs.

For, the enlightened, courteous and interested in foreigners, those with good enough manners not to force their beliefs and habits on strangers, who did not wish to blaspheme their religion, whatever, by using it as an excuse to grab an empire, are being forced to live by ''isms'. There is nothing left of geography. There is only history. The web of the present that forms the day-to-day of the town, of the dwelling in the land, the patient work of years of hum-drum small human actions, is stripped apart, macerated. A crude blunt finger has jabbed into the delicate tracery it cannot mend. The life of the present is pulped by the gormless boot of ideas of the past. Scornful Northern men are feeding on old sagas to keep themselves quarrelsome — sagas I once loved and now am sickened by, old sagas, old glory. There is shame only and no heroism in this pushing of people back to barbarism, back to baronry; shame only and lamentation, for the heroism has had its face slapped good and hard. It is too dull and quiet to be suitable as headlines for the modern saga-makers. It is giddy, it is concussed, it goes down under the boots, caught between the muscled thighs of the bullies bearing down from the opposing side and the desperate shoving of its own ranks behind it.

Of another city and another people was it lamented:

'She weepeth sore in the night and her tears are on
her cheeks;
Among all her lovers she has none to comfort her
All her friends have dealt treacherously with her
they are become her enemies.
. . . gone into captivity because of affliction and
because of great servitude
She dwelleth among the heathen, she findeth no rest
All her persecutors overtook her between the straits.'

Of what use is lamentation? No use. We lament the loss, the ruination of that which has been and is now destroyed. No use, but we lament. We call out loudly that we hate what has been done so that people may know that we mourn with them the destruction in them of the shoots of generosity, tolerance and enlightenment by the war machinery and bullying of benighted barbarians.

JENNY JOSEPH

ONCE THERE WAS A BRIDGE . . .

On Monday 8 November 1993 there was a death in my family. My telephone was ringing late into the night. From many distant places friends and acquaintances called to express their heartfelt sympathy. In the papers the next morning there were obituaries and photographs. They showed the dead looking youthful and in good health in spite of the burden of many years. It was not time for him to die. The death of a loved one always comes too soon but when death comes suddenly, unnaturally, the pain is deeper, more terrible and longer lasting.

Above the green waters of the River Neretva, mischievous as a foal and eternal as life itself, in deep old age and in the very place where he was born and where he lived for 427 dignified and graceful years, loving the river below him and making friends with all people, Mostar's oldest and most respected inhabitant was secretly and shamefully assassinated. The citizens of Mostar are fine swimmers but, last year, in the summer, it was those from beyond the Neretva's left bank, those who do not know how to swim, who first wounded the Old Bridge; and then he was to be wounded by the same kind of non-swimmer from the right bank: scrapers of the *gusle* on the one hand and howlers of *gangi* on the other. These gloomy people, evil, and used neither to bridges nor rivers nor to the towns from which they always shrink but which, when conditions permit, they plunder and then ruin and burn in order to cover their traces.

Not Paris where the Eiffel Tower makes love to the heavens, nor yet Rome where the sky lies down to rest on the dome of St Peters; not London where Big Ben chimes out the time we have left to us and warns us of our mortality, nor any other town is distinguished and identified by anything that has been built by the hands of men in the way that Mostar was distinguished and identified by this Bridge which somehow became known as the Old Bridge. This was Mostar's Old Bridge, but he was fresher and more youthful than all the other bridges of Mostar. In relation to them he was an elder brother although he had years enough almost to be their grandfather. Those other bridges were younger brothers who were slaughtered at his very threshold, before the eyes of those citizens of Mostar who loved them most. The dead were deeply mourned. Great is the justice of it, yet small the consolation, that all of them now rest in peace together in the waters of the Neretva. There they will remain for eternity in the embrace of one whom they loved throughout life, for bridges are the truest lovers under the infinite canopy of the sky.

Bridges are built so that men do not need to go roundabout. They are built so that men can go directly to wherever it is they want to go. Where bridges are, the banks reach out and shake hands with each other. Where bridges are, the banks become related to each other. Bridges are like the souls of dead rainbows turned to stone across the waters. No other building that man has thought out with mind and spirit has so much soul as a bridge and none is so faithful to man and to its neighbourhood. Bridges are the most human of buildings. Of all buildings, the bridge is man's closest relation. And then there could never be a bridge like this murdered bridge. Bridges are too often too much of a muchness but this bridge was like itself alone or like a crescent moon gazing down into the waters of the Neretva when the night was quiet and the moonlight soft. All bridges, whether their roots are of blood, of concrete, or of metal, attach themselves into the banks and grow from them. Only Mostar's Old Bridge sprang up and spent its life literally on a couplet:

This bridge was built like the arc of the rainbow.
Ah, God! Is its like to be found anywhere in the world?

From this was the inscription on the first stone placed as a foundation stone in the year 1557. It was the architect Hajrudin, bridge builder by profession and poet in spirit, who brought this Bridge, in head and heart, from his native Persia to Mostar. He carried it across trackless wastes and fathomless seas. He blistered his feet in the mountains and soaked them in the waters of many rivers. But it was only just here between the rocky slopes of the hill called Hum the mountain called Velez, here above the impetuous and secret water which he had never before seen, that he decided to build his dream. Thus his Bridge was not

153

just a stone path across the water, rather it was a weaving of sonnets in stone, the white, hand-cut, local limestone that they call tenelija, strung out and sung out across the Neretva. It was more poem than bridge.

In the year 1566, and on the very evening before the Bridge was freed from its scaffolding and formally handed over to the citizens, the former builder Hajrudin secretly left the town never to return. He would never see the Bridge. It is not known why he left. Was it that he was afraid to meet with his own special loved one, or was his fear that this too high and too slender dream of stone might come toppling down into the river, or again, was he jealous of the great work that would outlive him? All who came later and saw the Bridge stopped before it in wonder and surprise, captured by its spell. Poets sang about it, story tellers told stories of it, painters painted it; as for ordinary people, they behaved like ordinary people and walked across it. The first recorded writing about the Bridge was left by Evlija Celebija, lover of travel and recorder of his journeys, who wrote:

'Behold! Let it be known that I, Evlija, miserable and unfortunate slave of God, have seen and travelled across sixteen empires, yet never have I seen so high a bridge. It is thrown across with stones one to the other which rise into the sky.'

Travellers and unexpected guests wondered at it across the centuries. In the nineteenth century there were the writers of books of travel, Beaujour and Chaumette, and a century before them the Frenchman, Poullais, on his way to the East, stood before the bridge and wrote:

'Its construction is braver and broader than that of the Rialto Bridge in Venice, and yet is the bridge in Venice looked upon as a wonder.'

To the writer of these lines, from the whole anthology of bridges, these two bridges lay close to his soul, and the Nobel prize winner, Ivo Andric, dipped his pen in the ink-like waters of the Neretva and paid literary homage to the Old Bridge at Mostar.

Around the Bridge the people gather and the town grows. The Bridge is younger than its town. The first time that the town appears under the name of Mostar is 1 June 1474, during the parliament of the representatives of the Dubrovnik Republic, where it is debated what gift should be made to the Subasa of Mostar, Skender. It is not known what was given to the Subasa but it is known that the townsmen were given the name 'bridgers' (mostari) in their role as guardians of the first (wooden) bridge. Nor is it known for certain what name Hajrudin's Old Bridge took when it was young, but it is known for certain that the Bridge was not born old.

Throughout history the Bridge has been where the young people of Mostar pass through a famous rite of passage. They matriculated from the Bridge. Children, who are always in a hurry to grow up, would leap from the arch of the bridge into the water. After three or four seconds of precipitate and dangerous flight they would swim to the banks as adults. But other leapers from the Bridge were those young girls of Mostar, naïve and too lovely, fleeing from life and from unhappy love. In winter the seagulls arrived from the south. They came from Dubrovnik and Makarska. They would cruise around and under the Bridge, and poor children shared their bread with them. The seagulls, restless above the water, as though the banks were snowballing each other, would leave again with the coming of the first blossom. If these gulls beneath this northerly Bridge have 'travelled south' to reach it, then the Old Bridge at Mostar was the most southerly bridge in Europe. I prefer to believe the biological compass of the gulls rather than that of the cartographers who draw Mostar on the map to the North of Dubrovnik and Makarska.

Behold! This bridge is no more. Murdered and beneath the water, it lives on in the hearts of the people. I do not want these lines to read like an In Memoriam. Although the people of Mostar have long known the words: 'If, God forbid, something should happen to this Bridge, we would build another, even more beautiful, and even older', such a beautiful and old bridge can never again be created. But we can and we must — when the madness ends, and the madmen have been put into straitjackets cut from their respective national flags and the golden keys to the town have been returned to the real owners of Mostar — raise a monument to the Bridge, built on the same surviving foundation stone. A monument which in its gracefulness, its goodness and its dignity will be exactly like that which had been erected. It shall be built of the white, hand-cut local limestone that they call tenelija, like a sonnet over the water. This 'Young Bridge' will be cared for by the future conscience of mankind, while it grows up and becomes stronger, throughout the whole of its later life and when it grows old. But especially when it grows old.

This will be, I believe, the right and just thing to do.

MIŠO MARIĆ

Written in November 1993 in Exeter, England, as a refugee, and in that emptiness over the Neretva where once there was a bridge.

Addressed to all dead and surviving citizens of Mostar whose lives were built upon the Bridge's foundation, and to all friends of Mostar and friends of Bridges who know how to hear me.

CHICKENS

She stoops low into the coop,
makes wick and oil the centre
of shadows, her shawl shouldered
huge against the wall, wavering.
The pungent sleepiness of a place
slowed by the dripping of dregs.
Her bright face emerges, made long
by the light: clutched in her apron,
half-hidden, the soft glow of eggs.

* * *

They're always there: one-eyed extras, onlookers to the main characters we think ourselves to be. When feathers fly in argument, they scatter in the vanguard; if a favourite plate's dropped, a forbidden sack opened, they're always a few goose-steps ahead of the criminal. A kind of emphasis to our back-yard drama. Except that they're quick to forget.

Entertainment, too. For me: my grandchildren chasing them, bent-kneed, like so many Grouchos; for them: I bend round a plasticine neck, to thread it under a wing, and leave the hen standing there, seemingly decapitated. But there was that ghoulish afternoon when, with neck half-severed, one leapt clean from the cauldron, half-plucked, did a foot-slapping lap of honour round the marble floor. Staggered across the line of the grate.

* * *

How we giggle, with horror in our hearts, whenever the soldiers come. We throw ourselves onto the wire fence, watch them swagger past. Grandma calls us in, gives us such a beating. Each night she murmurs with the few old men and women left in the village. They use words we recognize, but don't understand.

Today two soldiers come to the old house. Grandma is in the fields. They slash open all the sacks, gulp down our little wine, are taking the hens too. They look funny chasing them, one hand on their rifle straps, stuffing them into a sack. We are angry. We protest, but the soldiers smile. Then they look at us, and look at us, until we are afraid. One of them tries to lift my skirt with his rifle. I am 14. Maria is 12.

That is when Grandma appears, from a gap in the wall behind them. She is running in short, funny steps, one arm raised, almost like a dancer. There is something glinting above her fist. She gets one of them with the sickle, slicing through his helmet strap, leaving a gash in his neck. She turns for the second, but he brings down his rifle, fells her like an autumn stalk. Blood trickles from Grandma's mouth into a little pool in the dust. The bumps in the sack squirm, then spew out. We cry.

The soldier points his gun at us for a long time, just stands there, gritting his teeth, until the other begins to moan. He inspects the neck, shouts at us, then presses a handkerchief over the wound. With great effort, he lifts the body onto his back. It is dripping blood like a pig. He lurches off, cursing us. We cannot speak. Run off into the mountains. All we have is the chickens, and eggs.

* * *

> With Grandma's chickens in tow, we left
> no stone unturned — each damp socket
> speckled with the brilliant capsules
> of larvae. Bright-eyed, unblinking,
> the hens jabbed at what had been
> unbroken night. Picked it clean.

MARIO PETRUCCI

OPTIMISM

I have a photograph which moves me deeply. I cut it from a newspaper not so long ago. An old man sits beneath a tree. The tree is old too. Both are marked by the passage of years. The old man's face is lined and sad. The tree is splintered by shell-fire and stripped of much of its bark. And yet the old man has leaned his bicycle against the tree and is playing his violin — the case open before him. His eyes are shut — his mind and soul immersed in the music he is creating. He would not notice if someone took money from the violin's case, yet it seems that he trusts they will not. As he gives beauty back to the passers-by, so they give succour to him.

The tree asks even less. Above its war-torn trunk the tree, ignoring its injuries, has brought forth leaves and flowers in abundance. Giving beauty to all who care to look, and shade to those who venture under its damaged branches. It asks for nothing, not even for war to go away. Behind them both, the old man and the tree, order prevails where once was war and hatred. Men and women walk the street without fear. Bottle banks, bicycles, potted shrubs and street signs represent peace and order. A young man in a white sweater looks towards the violinist in relaxed attitude.

For Bosnia, a future will come when a violinist can busk in the streets and young men wear casual clothes not uniform. When citizens can saunter from one shop to another without fear or cycle in a leisurely manner down the streets of the towns; when glass is recycled and not used to make weapons; a time when there is a future for a shrub in a pot or a child in its cradle. To achieve this, hatred must be torn out by its roots and bridges built to unite people wrenched apart by war.

The simplest bridge of all is made when we hold hands in friendship. We teach our children that to shake hands is polite. We teach them games in which to take part hands must be held; ring a ring of roses, oranges and lemons to name but two common British games. It is time we took our hands out of our pockets and began building new bridges for the sake of the world's future — our children.

JANIS PRIESTLEY

AN IDEA IN
POETRY

A WAR CHILD

Her pain comes searching for its face
To catch the hooded shutter's eye,
To shape the rictus of a cry
And pass for more than commonplace.
It howls towards the consequence
Of misery it can't escape,
One of a world of mouths that gape
At nothing that makes any sense.

The village she has left behind
Is lost outside this picture's frame
Which only shows her running blind
From where the trusted neighbours came
To what seemed safety of a kind
But could not take away her shame.

JOHN MOLE

AN IDEA OF BOSNIA

FOR THE AID WORKERS

A man remembers a doorway in Mostar,
how his mother and father passed through it,
how the postman delivered messages,
how flowers and gifts and even hopes
crossed the threshold.
Then they covered it over, planks to protect,
sandbags and small boulders to cover the place
where entrances and exits had always been possible.
A silence came to the doorway in the midst
of the terrible screeches of war.
Between the gaps eyes sometimes spied.
A parcel was passed. A message got in.
Sometimes the planks were prised apart
and a broken body was carried out.
Twice even dead ones. And those inside
now became aware of other things. From
outside the sound of a child crying.
Once a song. Another time screams.
And once a being passed right through
the planks and sandbags and stones. It was
a real person. It was a person of the future.
It was a spirit to make this possible.
A man remembers a doorway in Mostar
and all the things that must go out
before the angels can truly enter.

DAVID H. W. GRUBB

THE BABY'S ROOM

The baby's room contains a smile
a statue of a ballerina
a tiny rosary
and fifty fish afloat on a mobile,

at the baby's window chestnut leaves
spread their hands on the glass
like friends begging the baby
to come out and play,

on the baby's ceiling the sun rises —
and the baby tries to lick
the butter-yellow fingerprints
on its white cot

while the music box slung from the cot-bars
plays the only tune it knows:
O my little Augustine
all is gone, all is gone . . . .

The baby's room contains a mobile
a statue of a ballerina
a tiny rosary
a music box that no one sets going
and the baby's invisible smile . . . .

HELEN DUNMORE

NOT FOR THEM

Never
could disaster
like that happen to them.
They were right. It happened to their
children.

RAYMOND TONG

163

CROSSING THE BORDER

I am making a cake.
I would rather do almost anything else
but I need a place for these ingredients.

Elsewhere, another woman risks
a shell-gashed balcony to light a fire.
She guides a baby's thumb into its mouth.

My cake is made of dry and wet elements.
The god of the fleeting moment
blesses them into something new.

She has boiled pasta, a handful
for her family of four; a smear
of mustard. They call it soup.

This cake is made of such plenty
yet it will not rise.
I mean it as an offering

but how can it fit into a time
of bread in the wrong places,
of no — no more — nothing?

If I could, I would walk with it
across the map of Europe,
over bland pastels, wavering boundaries,

to where she's silent as a man says,
*I won't die of death, but of
Love For My City.*

*   *   *

Children come like sparrows to my table
flight upon flight; cold
fingers grasp the hard edge,
nails scrabbling for grains of sugar.

I eat my warm, rich food. Every day
they have a more migrant look.
Above them, the funeral bird
strops a complacent beak.

Sanity would turn time
back on itself, reel the children in,
to stack them
in vast ovarian warehouses, sleeping.

Let their next life be as meadow larks
— their high, clean thatness;
dying just deaths
unfreighted by love, pride, consequence.

CAROLE SATYAMURTI

CAUSE AND EFFECT

He thought before the war
Of conflicts, heroism, enemies
Who had to be crushed;
Causes that had to be fought for.

He had no time before the war
For bright skies, fields, the warm
Sun, his woman — only
Causes that had to be fought for.

I see him now after the war
In my lifetime. I notice his love
Of the sun, bright skies, fields, his woman:
Causes that have to be fought for.

ALAN BOLD

WHAT TUDOR SEES

There's a hole in the minaret
below the muezzin's balcony.
Through it,
Tudor spies the sky Mohammed made.
It's blue as a dream,
bright as a promise. Some place,
an eagle soars, the pigeons
unafraid of beaks and talons. The
high clouds now, at sunset,
have a pattern
like the Persian rug
his grandmother set her chair upon.

There's a hole in the spire
beneath the cast-iron bell frame.
Through it,
Tudor sees the clouds that Jesus rides.
They're white as ducks' down,
light as the hair-seeds drifting
from the dry flax heads
by the mill race. If he squints,
the ragged stones smooth over
and nothing seems amiss.

There's a hole in the wall
where once the window was,
Through it,
Tudor sees the old lady from No. 84
scuttle like a worried crab
for the cover of the burned-out Skoda.
Over the splintered oak hang
the grey puffballs of explosions.
Once, he saw a Tomcat
dive by just like the movies,
and he looked, but Tom Cruise
wasn't in the cockpit:
the rockets hit the primary school.

There's a hole in Tudor's head
Through it,
he sees a red kite bucking on thermals,
Uncle Valerian's donkey braying in an orchard,
Irina's kitten preening its whiskers,
Augustin skipping by the river,
his mother singing by the washtub . . .

. . . and his father oiling
an AK47.

And he wonders what's real
and what is not.

MARTIN BOOTH

GOING ON

The cemetery in Sarajevo
is fruitful and multiplying.
Long lines like winter wheat
limed with snow, each black stone blade
over the husks of lives. The grave-diggers
keep making furrows.
Here is too much silence
under the dead sky. But in the streets
quiet breaks in split seconds
when bullets enter uninvited
and leave their marks on walls
for you to show your friends:
'This is my first bullet, this the third.'

But a man dances under his umbrella
over the rainshone square. Celebrates.
Candles flicker where
people sit huddled round tables,
and women get pregnant, say
they will go on.

ANNE BORN

GAMBIT
FOR BOSNIA

To see a way
Through fire
And smoke

A way to love
The world we make
Makes good

PETER DENT

THE FRONT

He took a bullet
and fell.
I went down to him
ducked under their fire.

I have you
It's alright
I said.

Pulling his arms around my neck
I carried him back
to the safety of our line.
His face was wet against my neck.

They did not let up
the whole way.

Taking bullets all the while
he died against me
and I wore him
like pelt
my shield
my brother
my other skin.

TONY CURTIS

NO ONE TAKES A PROFIT

Powder snow falling on the town
And on the sea as I cycle home.
A kindly man peers at complex instruments
And is himself a focus of trust.
A small monthly direct debit
For whatever unspecified fear you have
Say being poor and alone in pain.
Applications by the stated deadline
For the single market or community
And best quality Turkish kidneys.
Easing model looks into a body scan,
I saw him in the furniture advert
Quizzical looks, good at looking
Quizzical. Was it a bomb shelter
Or a military command post?
A launch pad or a hospital?
The same look through optical equipment
At somebody's aged anxious aunty
All very shiny and technical.
My ears are full of snow tonight
Tyres print the snow as they run
Through Phear park to Green Close
Home. A small child's smile lights up.
Into this feeling the claws grip
And dig and wedge and separate:
You are either outside or in.
Hand in hand the children go
Barefoot ahead of the tanks
Into the Bosnian winter.

TONY LOPEZ

LET A THOUSAND BOSNIAN FLOWERS BLOOM

1. IRMA AND THE DIPLOMATS

Expedient, as well as moral,
this selection of a single little girl
out of the rows of the mortared;

with the low opinion polls
and the necessity for a statesman
to prove himself effective.

Easier than stopping the shrapnel
in the first place and inhumane
of anyone to say so.

* * *

2. EDITORIAL

So who was Irma?
By the time I printed this
she'd be forgotten

* * *

3. THE DIPLOMATS AT CHRISTMAS

Even without candles
there would be risks,
if not of conflagration:

old lights set flickering
on a new-cut tree
already moulting needles.

With a lightening of days
there ought to be
an end to harrowing:

cold roses at least,
climbing like spires
out of a stubborn bed.

Always a chequered gambit,
this adversarial quadrille
confined by precedent:

so here we sit
trying to play chess
with our backs to the open window . . .

* * *

4. EDITORIAL (Two)

Vague and generalized:
you must be more specific,
to be effective!

* * *

5. EPILOGUE

Through postal cross-fire,
a bubble reputation?
Try heavier mortars!

DAVID GOODALL

SOUVENIR FROM ZAGREB

As I play my Serbo-Croat double flute,
the first few double notes in rising scale
walk out like married couples from a church
in loving unison.

But four stops on the Serbian pipe don't match
the Croat three, and soon no earthly skill
can keep the two in harmony. Too late:
Dubrovnik's ancient battlements dissolve
beneath the Serbian shell.

DAVID GILL

FLESH MARKETS

We are traders too of a sort, from a safe distance.
We watch the pictures, we pay a little gelt
for our sensations and our feasting: these folk give
    themselves
without knowing, to those they cannot see.

(No, it is not a consolation, knowing
that if this is to be any kind of elegy, it is bound
to be forged from strangers' pain.)

Their streets are the broken trestles
where they display their wares:
it hurts them but they cannot stop,
they barter flesh for bullets,
they exchange their own meat for fire,
hoping for more land, or restored land. This is not
what we usually mean by a market.
It is not difficult to imagine the smell
that rises among the fumes of desolation.
Those with longish memories will talk of
the knacker's yard, the reek of the glue factory.

What is it about this feud that sucks back
the old words out of the mists —
massacre, carnage, slaying and slaughter,
battue, pogrom, a *noyade* in their own juices?
(There is a fearful relish in their taste on the
    tongue.)

Over there the butchers
cannot shut up shop now they've started,
there in the smoke-filled villages and towns
of a green and reeking land; we here cannot take
our eyes off what lies through the seemingly
unclosable doors of the shambles
that happens to be there, not here,
not on this particular pavement.

RODNEY PYBUS

ON WHAT ISLAND?

On what island shall we hold the party?
On a dead fish floating in the river?
On a ball bouncing along the motorway?
On a planet rolling in space?

On what island shall we hold the party?
On a sceptred isle with spoils privately?
On a video replaying the World Cup for ever?
On a Bosnian child's head?

On what island shall we hold the party?
On a poem balancing on the page?
On Atlantis?
On purpose?

DAVID HART

CARTOGRAPHY

The fresh proposal and the redrawn plan
Add and subtract a line from the torn map.

Sheer terror knows no enclave, it breaks free
To crack each boundary with its stubborn head

Around the table, giving grudging inch
Opposed, gridlocked, entrenched and staring out

Starvation recognizes no frontier
For nameless child of mothers of each side.

Our late news filters through the drag of guns
Intransigence prolongs the miles of death

Republic, separatist, and settlement
The signal fades towards the shrugging west

A map of crumpled paper now defines
Where blood has soaked along a nation's lines.

JOHN CALVERT

THE SONG OF THE REFUGEE CHILD

I may be little but let me sing,
I may be a child but let me in.
What does it matter if I read or write?
You'll send me to war to learn to fight.

I am the refugee child.

I am the hungry of a hundred lands,
mine is the blood that stains the white sands,
but I'll climb your barbed wire and walls of stone
and find a free place to make a new home.

I am the refugee child.

I am the dispossessed, wandering one,
you can't kill me with your bomb and your gun.
I am the face that looks out from the night
towards your rich window with its warmth and its
       light.

I am the refugee child.

I am a child of the family called Poor
And I am coming to knock on your door.
I may be little but let me sing,
I may be a child but you must let me in.

I am the refugee child.

ROBIN MELLOR

THOUGHTS OF RESISTANCE

Sometimes
I win wars
alone.

RUPERT M. LOYDELL

DIVIDING THE WORLD

As usual there weren't enough atlases.
'Share one between two,'
led to tugs back and forth
across our pushed-together desks.
But it was important to have
just a quarter of an inch more than her
especially as we were looking at South America
which was on her side that morning
and she wouldn't let me lean across.
From a distance it could have been
a green bunch of grapes,
some already turning purple,
dangling on page sixteen.
When I craned my neck to find
the source of the Amazon
she stabbed her heel into my toe
so I threw back my head and gave her chin
such a crack that Miss Owl said if we didn't behave
she'd really bang our heads together,
give us something to shout about.
So I whispered, 'You've got dirty hair
and fleas and I wouldn't come near you
for all the tea in China.'
At playtime her sister was waiting
in pointed shoes, black patent leather.
She kicked and a bruise
began to spread between my legs.
I couldn't wait to get home and tell my mother
who'd been at school with Miss Owl.
In the same class.

MARY MAHER

THE TRUCE

Another dawn with black trees
a warlike dawn where negotiations
have broken down
between all parties

earphones hang from the necks
of exhausted translators

dawn of silence, but for the
creak of empty escalators

Once words were at home
in this city
mischievous, they rustled
like children's feet on the stairs

they were snapdragons our fingers
rifled in the blue garden

The demagogues have frozen
our words to the walls

Now only the wind moves
in an agony of remembering,

and the flags on the rooftops,
the terrible white flags

ALISON FELL

ABANDONING THE MOUNTAIN

It was distance deceived you.
Clamber down to where seared turf
hummocks the site of old sills

and the firm outlines blur,
thistles stooping alarmed
over armed shadows of strangers.

Folded back under earth,
the hands that terraced layered silence
leave shattered tile and evergreen.

Chatter of birds is for valleys,
rightly far from the perch
of stoney alleys so severe,

the heart's counting-houses
that ledge and ledger exile, their abacus
quitted at a final reckoning.

Cloud pennants shake free
from the highest points,
beckoning inland off scarp and crest.

As you look downslope it seems
the dead are setting out to trespass
over the barbed wire of the living.

YANN LOVELOCK

THE BURN

Putting the honey to warm on the boiler
to soften it for his slice of toast
and feeling the blessed heat on his face
this cold morning he must have reached out
his hand, instinctively drawn to the vibrant
silver flue.

　　I'd sooner not think
of his fingers like solder, his speechless pain
that brought us running from separate rooms
to soothe him with hydrocortisone cream
and a timely bandage wrapped round and round.
No hockey. No rock guitar class. No flute
for a week at least.

　　But though it still hurts —
he's taken painkillers with him to school —
it's already healing, won't scar, won't be
remembered at all by the end of the war.

MICHAEL LASKEY

UTTERANCE

When hurt why do we cry out still?
What utterance once softened pain,
once staunched the blood-loss from a vein,
once threw predators off the kill?

— Evolution's treachery
to utilize the weak in death?
(Some creature's only voice is breath.)
Dear, we must cry more quietly.

PETER DALE

SQUARE 7e

And he had peace of mind But
the world was not at peace The
thought disturbed him He began
to   feel   guilty,   to   feel   that
his   peace   alienated
him from the world He lost his
peace but could not lose the guilt

GERALD ENGLAND

REMEMBER ME

not the flies crawling over my skin,
not the begging bowl in my hand,
not the burden on my shoulders,
not the disease, not my elders,
not the chants, the dance, the gestures,
not the charity, poses, lectures,
not the journalists, the convoy's drive,
not the image, not the rhyme,
not the agony in my mother's womb,
not the rotting of my father's tomb,
not the cliché, myth or blistering,
not the silence, not the posturing,
not the ghost of my broken home,
not the thinking of your own,
and the guns, not the savagery,
not the blind eye, nor immunity,

if you look
remember ME
    throat dry
stomach empty

ANTHONY ROLLINSON

READING LESSON

A is for aeroplane
B is for bomb
M is for man
Here is a baby
here is a bomb
B is for baby and bomb

Here is a woman
holding her baby
Here is a man
with a gun in his hand
H is for hand

W is for world
spinning in space
it is round like a ball
B is for ball
also for baby and border
This invisible line
is a border
and around it is country
C is for country
Maybe you were born here
B is for born
and for baby, remember?

B is for border
and ball
C is for country
Are you comfortable?
C is for comfortable

What does it mean?
It means
B for bed
F for food
H for house
W for water
Without these it is not comfortable
Are you comfortable?

If you cross the invisible line
B for border
you may find yourself
in someone else's country
C is for country

Perhaps the man with the gun
lives there
M for man
G for gun
He may not want you to stay
He may fire his gun

Perhaps he has no house
no bed
no food
no water
W for water and world
He is not comfortable
neither are you

Bullets fly
so do bombs
remember B for both
They fly like birds
another B
and cross invisible borders
and large countries
very easily
where people
P for people
are not always comfortable

But this is history
beginning with H
like hand
so we will close the book
B for book
and I will give you a biscuit
What letter does biscuit begin with?

ANNE BERESFORD

PICTURES OF BOSNIA

When I was young we played at war.
We gloried in the battle's roar.
Our weapons — only make believe;
We'd shoot with fingers, stoop and heave
Our hand grenades — just bits of wood;
Perhaps we'd stop to see who could
Die best, the most dramatic, like,
Then hurry home by foot or bike
At lunch time, 'cos us soldier-kids
Ate meals the size of dustbin lids.
But always, always, back we came
To finish off our deadly game.

It was, therefore, a culture shock
That distant war, that barren rock.
When TV pictures, framed by sound,
Showed huddled bodies on the ground.
Instinctively, I had a hunch
They'd not be going home for lunch.

PHIL CARRADICE

IN THE QUEUE FOR WATER
Sarajevo, December 1992.

They come with blistered saucepans.
They come with kerosene tins.
Nobody has a plastic bucket
as new and blue and fine as mine.

> Oh, my grandmother's samovar,
> my mother's wine glasses,
> my American Pyrex!

The soles of their shoes are like paper.
Their stockings are lumpy with darns.
Nobody here has leather brogues
as polished and brown and fine as mine.

Oh, my grandfather's riding-boots,
my father's Oxfords,
my Italian shoes!

Most jackets have lost their buttons.
Collars and cuffs are frayed.
Nobody has a full-length coat
as dark and woollen and fine as mine.

Oh, my grandmother's crochet shawls,
my mother's tweed ensembles,
my British raincoat!

Watches have vanished for flour,
necklaces melted to grease.
Nobody has a bracelet of gold
as heavy and twisted and fine as mine.

Oh, my grandmother's rubies,
my mother's wedding ring,
my Swiss diamonds!

Scarves are as thin as bandages.
Colours are scrubbed away.
Nobody has a white fox fur
as cunning and warm and fine as mine.

Oh, my grandmother's Persian lamb,
my mother's ermine stole,
my Russian mink!

* * *

I am thinking: perhaps I was conceived
the night before the Archduke's carriage
brought him to this town.

ADÈLE GERAS

BOY

They cannot cope with him,
The boy who terrorises other children.

When war came
And all the men went off to fight
The boy was left to guard the village.
They gave him a gun
And said, 'If strangers come,
You shoot them, right?'
He nodded.
He was fourteen.
Late one night
A man stole from the darkness.
Then the boy thought of his promise,
His responsibility.
He aimed, shut his eyes tight
And shot the man
Who was his father. Now
They cannot cope with him,
The boy who terrorises other children.

SUE COWLING

EUROPEAN GAMES

Remembering the agony and triumph,
The three perform the medal ceremony
As if it were a sporting version of
The Crucifixion or Transfiguration,
And like a Christmas tree with chocolate money,
The solemn victor wears his decoration,
The gold he plundered from the enemy.
Three flags ascend to his national anthem,
A brassy dance tune. In the setting sun
The shadows of the flags all look the same.

DUNCAN FORBES

HOW IT HAPPENS

One night's enough.
The shut shop's lights go off

for the last time. By dawn
it's done.

The window's been flypostered
over and over — some no-hoper

local band's first gig, a Socialist Worker
SMASH THE something X'd out with a swastika —

like a crumpled letter lost
years in the post

with ranks of stamps in small
denominations, all the same half-smile:

the crown prince of somewhere nobody's
heard of except quiet boys

with specs and Stanley Gibbons
catalogues, deep in the innocence

of watermarks and first-day covers
and the sound of words like *Bosnia-Hercegovina*.

Quaint name. Then it's not.
It happens. Just like that.

PHILIP GROSS

'OUR HISTORY WAS LIKE A DESERTED STREET'

— *DMITRI VOLKOGONOV*

The parade with flags and cheering faces
passes across a scratched newsreel
in silence. No echo was caught on the soundtrack.
Events that mattered took place offstage.
Machine-guns stuttered from distant squares.

Families in that grey block of flats
were all taken. Some screamed for mercy.
Most went in sullen obedience. One by one
the little shops closed down.
The postman became a rare visitor.
No one wanted to set down the past.

They shut the newsagent's. Then the library.
Perhaps, behind that neo-classical façade,
the books are still gathering dust.
Probably not. They'll have been destroyed
along with the archives, for history
must be a series of blank chapters.
Those who could have testified will never come
    back.

It's not a street now for the living. Bare pavements.
Bare roadway. No hoardings or bicycles.
Uncurtained windows. Windows boarded up.
Smashed windows betraying darkness,
glass splinters glittering in the gutter.

The men and women who belonged here,
who bought their bread and cigarettes
and waited for trams chatting by the kerb
lie tossed in an unmarked pit.
Some ended as cold smoke

spewed from chimneys above the ovens.
Others sprawl as bones
among a handful of metal name-tags
in a ditch near the battlefield.

It took a lot of lead —
and chemicals — and paperwork.
It took determination as well as an unswerving
loyalty to the cause. It took time.
It took shoe-leather and medals
and throats gone hoarse from shouting orders.
It took cordite — and barbed wire —
and the axe-blade. It took persuasion.
But in the end it proved worth the trouble.
The street lies deserted.
It need never be peopled again.

HARRY GUEST

SMOKING IN SARAJEVO

Old friend, the flaw was planted even then,
your thumb-nail khaki from the tobacco
as you climbed into the stolen jeep, though
she had clung to your shirt-sleeve, the button
left in her hand. And with entrenched men,
silenced by approaching thunder, it drew
something from nothing — a means to endow
hands and mouth with their own remembering.
Is that it? Were you suckling forgetfulness?
Or did you hear her, calling through the smoke;
see her, falling in the market, face blue,
a flagstone spattered with her water, eggs,
flour; feel her clutch at her belly, revoke
all strength to the absent sky, want you?

MARIO PETRUCCI

VEDRAN SMAILOVIC

People dash across our TV screens
like sheep scatting from a moorland blaze,
they'll disappear over the edge of dreams
when we ascend to sleep away the day.

But, all of a sudden, within a frame,
a portrait animated and tightly-strung:
the cellist plays on streets where lame
buildings hobble before falling down.

His slashback hair is ageing rocker style,
his upturned moustache makes a sign of peace;
his two faces: a pizzicato smile
and mournful vibrato of so much grief.

His audience are the pavement wreaths,
from the distance come heckles of gunfire:
the amphitheatre where he once bowed
is a frozen skip of bricks and wires.

On a thin point he gradually spins
the web-fine veins of an Adagio,
while hearing the bombs' deadening dins
and fearing for that small bridge below.

MIKE JENKINS

FOR NERMA

Who lives in her apartment now?
And do they keep the door ajar
For all the neighbours' children
As she used to do?
Who plays her piano?
Do their fingers stroke the harmonies just so?
She'd like to know.
She understands the language here
But sees the way we look at her sometimes
And wonders just exactly what she's said.

She feels her dreams move in her sleeping head
And thinks of home where other dreamers
Dream in that same tongue that once she heard
The stories of her childhood in.
The people here are kind,
She tries so hard, she almost doesn't mind
The way the clothes in binbags tend to smell —
They'll wash. And she says thank you
For each little thing. Discreetly throws away the
        dross
She won't offend the giver — they're the boss.
They mean so well. But she has learned —
She's half worn out with being grateful
Would like to be the giver now and then.
Feels pain. Feels loss.

JAN DEAN

SEPTEMBER, BEGINNING OF THE WINTER

As I saw the bright remains of the fire extinguishing
        foam
which was hugging the burnt skeleton of the
        neighbouring skyscraper
with the confidence of snow, suddenly I felt
an abandonment, which can only be compared with
the destiny of a coin withdrawn from circulation.

This year, reality quotes its price
condescendingly — like a tradesman, imperceptibly
        it casts
a shadow like that left on a smoker's lungs
by a scrounged cigarette.

IGOR KLIKOVAC

A THREE-WAY SPLIT . . .

the weatherman looks sunny.
But east of Split
the line would not sound funny.
In theory, cakes
and apples may be cut
with very few mistakes
occurring, but
countries are not
cakes or apples. Lives
do not as easily relate
to knives
slicing through communities.
The war

thrives upon disunities,
the scar
provided when the blade
incises skin.
When the maps were made
the artist's pen
was poised as if about
to sever flesh.
Soon a direct hit
upon a crèche
brings the dead cartography
to life.
A husband claws at bricks to free

his wife
and only child.
The weatherman is easy.
'The north may well be wild,
the west coast breezy,
but further south, in fact,
things seem quite good.'
The worst that will afflict
this neighbourhood

is intermittent showers
of English rain.
In Tuzla, hours
of shelling start again.

PAUL GROVES

THE LONG REACH OUT OF WAR

They will keep restoring the glass
in broken cathedrals

to carry the eye and the colours
that were shattered

They will keep restoring the stone
in bombed cathedrals

to carry the face and the idea
that were crushed

They will keep carrying the burden
of destroyed cathedrals

even as the ashes blow back

Humanity
keeping faith with itself
even as the ashes blow back

KATHERINE GALLAGHER

A RIDDLE FOR THE SERBIAN WARS

I am smoke curling from the cannon's mouth
a cockerel's white feather

I am the cry of women the keening
shell that falls into a town's sleep

I am the roof beams burning
and the cellar's huddled dark

I am the poem in a rapist's mouth
the rictus of hanged men

I am this hushed breathing
this shrinking prayer this litany of lies

I am the speck in a neighbour's eye
that covets your thistled acre

I am a white eagle a white dove
a white face pressed to the wire

I am the sudden knock at your door
the torchlight checking your face

I am the soldier's unsheathed pride
the slurred song of a nation

I am the cartographer drunk on ink
my hand on the pen the trigger the pulse

I am the question glinting at the border
the black stamp across your name

I am a dumb witness a twisted tongue
a language pecked out and sung by crows

Who am I?

GRAHAM MORT

THE MOSQUE AT CAZIN
(Cazin, 3.8.84)

In the market a hundred feet below
there are women selling Bosnian lace,
men sifting iron bolts and shackles,
bales of greasy wool in stacks,
melon slices, peaches, prunes
and flies. An agreeable heat
melts ice, but never reticence,
for the stout, pantaloon-clad matrons
of the faith sprawled in the shade.

A narrow road winds steeply round
the hill up to the white-minareted
mosque. Men in black skull-caps,
soberly and uniformly dressed, are in
its yard. There is a courteous welcome
for the hatless infidels who, shoes off,
wearing shorts and summer tops,
are admitted to a quiet sanctuary
of rugs and reverently upheld palms.

It is a mosque in which no local
women are allowed to worship. There
are curious stares at these bronzed
legs and arms. On our return down
the rough hill more stares and then
a smile. Salaam. A handshake
given with true warmth and amity.
Two strangers, he and I, meet
for a brief instant on the hill.

JEFFERY WHEATLEY

LIVING IN REAL TIMES
(Summer, 1993)

In Queen St, Cardiff, I halt to watch in a choice
of screens an over of the Trent Bridge Test,
Shane Warne looping wristspin in at
some tailender doomed at best to timeserving

till stumps. Between padded-off balls the eye
    flickers
to the other channel banked in
other sets, headlines unspooling soundless
beyond Curry's window, the newsreader's
    mouthings:

a street elsewhere foreshortened
by the long lens. Someone running in the tottering
apologetic way the very frightened run,
as if to panic and sprint could only serve

unfailingly to draw the sniper's bullet. Now
someone whom that bullet has already found. He
    lies
sprawled amid the usual crazed, cradling women
like one adored at last beyond all dreams.

Sarajevo? Mostar? Vukovar? . . . TV's intimate and
generalising eye makes everywhere somewhere else:
a province of that small, remote country
of which we, famously, know little

still. While post-modernism makes all things
present, all things post-reality (from the intensity
of this particular and very private grief I realize
I saw these shots two hours ago). Again

the street, down which no doubt the dead man too
had run. Past those same bins, the burned-out
truck, between the building's cover and
a water standpipe. Running partway

then throwing his hands up at it all
and falling dead just at that piece of broken kerb . . .
As he falls over and over again now in the women's
keening, or in some syndicated twenty-second

filmclip replayed over the next day's news.
Night-time, street, streetlight, a chemist's shop,
wrote Alexander Blok as Russia came apart
(that is, the first time round):

Whatever you come to, wherever
you go, it all comes down at last
to this. *You'll die, and just as always start
the dance again.* Over and over. And forever

and for ever. No *Amen.* While from the other end,
on another set, Merv Hughes — that moustache
bigger than Nietzsches's — takes the wicket,
a jubilant slip hurling high the catch, fieldsmen

throwing up their hands, the hangdog batsman
turning away, reluctant as a stood-up groom:
live now, sudden, in real time.
And I wait automatically, lingering

to watch them all do it again, in slowmo,
almost missing it the first time,
trained to the instant replay and the freezeframe:
to the destined fact, knowing there's no way out.

DUNCAN BUSH

TO THE ISLAND
for the Albanian poet Natasha Lako

This is when I would go out to the island:
before the heat, in the early morning —
its grove was the centre of my thoughts.
At dawn I would walk down,
upsetting sparrows in conversation
after dreams, hopping among puddles,
fluttering among chalices of elderberries.

But that would be in England, when autumn
mints Mediterranean dawns.
Behind the frontier you are bright-eyed,
lying in wait for me; and I will
see what I can do by letters
of protest, by arousing public
opinion. Now let me get back to

the conical hills. To my island.
Blackberries were jet and hips rubies.
They looped like minuets on a feathered
dance floor of branches; underneath
there lingered a macrocosmic
garden of weeds and grasses
still in ferocious gold-green harmony.

I lingered in the dew between two
galleries hung with the abstracts
of spiders, with cabinets of porcelains,
brambles, ivories, mayweed, peepshows,
vetches. I cast off, a mandarin
hooking ivory spillikin oars over
waves you never move or disturb —

You write in broken English, jubilantly
dishevelled, passionate, throwing
out cries for assistance and rejections
of same in consecutive undated notes,
refusing my request for a steady
address, perhaps in the revolution
there is none. I return, baffled.

I went for the quay, my boat
scraped on northern stones magisterially
furred with the past (kings, earls
and formal liberties taken by thatchers),
I could not hear the jubilant
voice of the oak, the ash or the thorn
except in hallucinations pre-dawn.

So I keep up with you, my dear friend,
in broken languages, in sympathy.
The weeds are engraved with the rubbing
of a brass tomb, with my footprints
drawn to the cool island.
You pull me into disastrous cities,
crying and laughing and crying.

JUDITH KAZANTZIS

GLOBE LIGHT

Today
he has killed me
with his guns
until he tires of that game
and says
You're better now
and I believe him

tonight I search the room
for monsters
have to look
under the bed
face my lack
of housework
dust can settle
in this house

— the world at his hand
he lights it with a flick
of a switch
It makes me safe
he says
What are those lines?
I try to explain
how countries start
and finish

his night light shines
a world away

LOUISE HUDSON

THE WAR PROCESS

Ceasefire planned   Ceasefire coming
Talks planned   Peace broker coming
Talks postponed   Ceasefire broken.

Mediators in place   Deadline imposed
Tuff negotiations   Tension grows
Negotiations breakdown.   Deadline goes.

Ceasefire planned   UN repeats
Talks on talks talked   UN repeats
Airport taken.   UN repeats.

UN debates   Mediators in place
Resolutions made   Foothill taken
Deadline imposed.   Talks breakdown.

Deadline coming   UN debates
Reinforcements coming   Factions debate
Deadline gone.   Factions won't budge.

Massacre discovered   Ceasefire planned
Cover-up uncovered   Ceasefires come
Hard line taken.   Ceasefires go.

Refugee talk.

My Rwandan friend said,
'At least they have ceasefires in Bosnia.'

My Bosnian friend said,
'What is a ceasefire,
by the way?'

BENJAMIN ZEPHANIAH

Вече На Шкољу

Пучина плава
Спава,
   Прохладни пада мрак.
Врх хриди црне
Трне
   Задњи румени зрак.

И јеца звоно
Боно,
   По крму дрне звук;
С уздахом туге
Дуге
   Убоги моли пук.

Клече мршаве
Главе
   Пред ликом Бога свог—
Ишту. Ал' тамо,
Само
   Ћути распети бог.

И сан све ближе
Стиже,
   Прохладни пада мрак.
Врх хриди црне
Трне
   Задњи румени зрак.

Алекса Шантић   1911

Evening on the Island

Azure, the ocean
Slumbers,
   As coldly falls the dark.
The high black clifftop
Quenches
   The final fiery spark.

The hollow tocsin
   Whispers,
   And shivers from hillside bare;
Sighs, born of endless
Sorrows,
Voice the suffering peoples' prayer.

Hollow-cheeked throngs are
Kneeling
   By God's image long adored—
Beseeching. But only
Silent
   Hangs the crucified Lord.

And sleep comes ever
Nearer,
   As coldly falls the dark.
The high black clifftop
Quenches
   The final fiery spark.

Translated by Yvonne Burns 1991

Veče na Školju

Pučina plava
Spava,
   Prohladni pada mrak.
Vrh hridi crne
Trne
   Zadnji rumeni zrak.

I jeca zvono
Bono,
   Po kršu drće zvuk;
S uzdahom tuge
Duge
   Ubogi moli puk.

Kleče mršave
Glave
   Pred likom Boga svog—
Ištu. Al' tamo,
Samo
   Ćuti raspeti Bog.

I san sve bliže
Stiže,
   Prohladni pada mrak.
Vrh hridi crne
Trne
   Zadnji rumeni zrak.

Aleksa Šantić   1911

Aleksa Šantić (1868-1924) lived most of his life in his native town of Mostar, and is considered one of the outstanding Serbian poets of the early part of this century.
Yvonne Burns

AN IDEA FROM FIELD REPORTS

SARAJEVO
A Shattered City

by GORDON BACON
FEED THE CHILDREN
CROATIA/BOSNIA AND HERCEGOVINA
AUTUMN 1993

Looking out of the window of the French Air Force Hercules transport plane as it approached Sarajevo airport, there was no doubting you were in a war zone. Every house I could see as we neared the runway was gutted. Ours was the only aircraft on the ground. The pallets of food had been unloaded, the five other passengers and myself hurried across the apron to the safety of the sandbagged, but badly shot up terminal building.

I got a lift with Gary Sullivan, UNHCR's transport

chief, whom I had met in Zagreb a few months earlier. He pointed out an armoured Land Rover waiting to be taken to Zagreb for repairs. It was in that vehicle a few days earlier that a UNHCR driver had been killed in Vitez. He was hit by an armour-piercing round which passed through the vehicle's armour, then through the back and front body armour plates as well as his body. It then lodged in the vehicle's protected windscreen. Not exactly a welcoming sight, especially when the local driver of our soft-skinned Nissan Patrol told us the Serb front line was just 100 metres away!

Driving into the town was like watching a movie from World War II. Virtually every building was damaged, many were completely destroyed, even massive tower blocks.

I visited a few people at the UNHCR office and then set off for the only operating hotel, the Holiday Inn. The driver, knowing it was my first visit to the city centre, gave me some good advice that I was happy to take, 'Do not leave the hotel other than in a vehicle, there are many snipers in the area.' He knew his geography and in certain areas he accelerated, saying snipers would shoot at anything, including clearly marked UNHCR vehicles.

I entered the hotel from a rear door away from the sight of the Serb gunmen. The hotel was busy; the media of the world were there covering the evacuation of the sick and injured who needed treatment in other countries. The Sarajevo doctors have the skills to treat all ailments but shortage of consumable supplies and the uncertain and extremely poor electricity supply make major, and often lengthy operations impossible.

I had travelled into Sarajevo to meet David Williams of The Daily Mail following the launch of the newspaper's second appeal to assist Feed the Children to help the children of Sarajevo and central Bosnia.

I had to climb the stairs to my bedroom on the eighth floor. Once inside I realized the window was thick plastic covering broken glass. One side of the head-board was scarred with shrapnel damage. It crossed my mind that I hoped the saying 'lightning doesn't strike in the same place twice' was true!

It was a hot day and the climb with my luggage and flack jacket left me with a thirst, so it was back down the eight flights to the bar in the lobby. I ordered a glass of orange and a bottle of beer. The orange was awful and the beer, I now know, was made from rice, and was disgusting!

When Dave Williams arrived at the hotel I was introduced to his driver, Jano, who was a Croat. He owned a coffee bar with his wife, who was a Muslim, and they employed two Serbs to run the bar. They all just wanted the war to end so that they could get on with their lives. I later learned that 40 per cent of marriages in Sarajevo this year were mixed race marriages.

The following day Jano took me to the two main hospitals, the State Hospital and Kosavo Hospital. As we arrived at the State Hospital, a private car drove to the casualty entrance. Amid a scrum of people I saw a young man being taken from the back of the car and placed on a stretcher. He had a gaping wound in his forehead. He had been hit by a sniper and although I heard he was alive when he was admitted, I would think he probably died from his wound.

There were not, thankfully, too many children in the hospitals. Many had already been evacuated to other countries. I did, however, see some children who needed to be evacuated to have any chance of a complete recovery.

At the entrance to the children's ward at Kosavo Hospital was a sign saying 'Djeca Remaja Hranu' (No baby food). It was a good feeling to know that I was going to be able to do something to help that situation.

Driving round the city with Jano, I saw people everywhere in queues for water. I was surprised at the number of them moving about in the streets. I was told, however, that it was at times like these that one shell would kill twenty people.

I met a family living in a school classroom. Halil Banda, his wife, mother and three children (aged 6, 9, and 12), had lived there for fourteen months after their home, which was situated on the front line, had been partially destroyed.

At the time of my visit petrol was £54 a gallon, diesel was £27 a gallon, and a can of Budweiser beer was £6.

It was incredible to think there were almost half a million people still living in Sarajevo, and I was surprised to see so many children. Yet unlike the blitz in the cities of the United Kingdom during World War II — when children were evacuated to country areas — there were no easy escape routes for the children of Sarajevo.

To assist me in assessing the situation quickly from Feed the Children's point of view, I had meetings with the officers from UNHCR, UNICEF, WHO (World Health Organization), and the French Organization, AICF.

The result of these meetings left me feeling that Feed the Children should try to help Sarajevo with aid but not personnel. The other agencies had people on the ground, apart from the Serb-controlled areas, which were too dangerous to cover on their own. I agreed that Feed the Children would assist the children of Sarajevo with baby food through UNICEF and with medical assistance through WHO.

The agencies are in place in Sarajevo and very well co-ordinated. I left there feeling that if Feed the Children had the resources to increase its manpower, it should be in central Bosnia where the needs are even greater.

EXCERPT FROM FAX
November 1993

RECEIVED FROM MALCOLM TURNER
FTC FIELD DISTRIBUTION TEAM, VITEZ, BOSNIA

' . . . It was the morning of Sunday, 7 November 1993 when she came to see us; a young mother with a baby in her arms. The baby, a 1-year-old girl with a terrible skin complaint. The poor little mite was covered from head to toe with angry red blotches and was obviously in a great deal of discomfort. I could see the mother was in tears and her own distress was evident.

With her was an older man I took to be her father. He spoke to me through our interpreter, Monica. The young woman, who looked to me to be no more than 20 years old, was already a widow, her husband lost in the war that ravages the ill-fated country. This child had suffered acutely from what I guessed to be eczema or psoriasis for six months, half its life. And now over-burdened by its suffering, the child was refusing to eat. The poor woman, having lost her husband, now faced the prospect of losing her daughter. My heart reached out to the distraught young mother as she held tightly to the whimpering bundle.

Denied access, by war, to proper medical advice, she had come to me in desperation. She knew that Feed the Children had worked hard to help beleaguered children in both warring camps, Croat and Muslim, and had established a reputation for helping wherever possible.

But neither I nor my partner, Craig Spencer, are doctors. We drive trucks and administer the distribution of baby food, so what could we do?

The mother was pressing us to transport the child to the town of Zenica, a Muslim-held town where there was a hospital. She, as a Croat, knew there were great dangers in such an idea, but she had reached such depths of despair that she was prepared to go to any lengths to secure the survival of her sickly child. On the other hand, I knew that she stood little chance of realizing her hopes; others before had tried and had failed. As gently as I could, I explained this to her, finding it difficult to cope with her painful expression of disappointment.

I could not present her with merely a shrug of the shoulders. I resolved to do what I could as best I could, as a person untrained in these matters. I asked what I thought were relevant questions about the child's weight and general condition, and with these details, together with my own imperfect observations, I crossed the road into the Army Camp here in Vitez. I asked to see the MO (army doctor).

Colonel Jackson of the RAMC was very polite. As a doctor he was clearly here to help, but the examination and treatment of Bosnian civilians was strictly outside his remit. 'But,' I argued, 'could you not, from the description I gave, at least give me some advice?' Patiently he explained that no doctor could make a proper diagnosis without an examination; the possibilities for getting it wrong were too great. I understood that, but my understanding of Colonel Jackson was not going to help baby Vanja.

I persisted, 'Look, I have a distressed mother come to me for help, I have neither the training nor the resources to provide that help. You, on the other hand, do, and so naturally I came to you. I know you are constrained by higher authority, but can't you, man to man, give me some advice?'

'I'll tell you what I'll do,' he said. 'The proper way to deal with this is to take it through GS, the section that deals with civilian matters and see if they can do something.'

The next day I was in the GS office talking to Sergeant Paul Murray. Talking was perhaps not an accurate term for I was receiving a dressing down for subverting the chain of command. I accepted the reprimand meekly, then asked, 'So what is going to happen to the little child?'

Sergeant Murray is, for all the toughness of his soldierly exterior, as soft as I am. When it comes to the suffering of a child, he was prepared to bend the rules and stretch a point. With might and main he strenuously worked to get Vanja in front of a qualified practitioner. He encountered obstacle after obstacle, which by persistence he overcame, and by the end of the week his persistence brought its reward when the child was examined by a paediatrician at a Muslim checkpoint some 15km from Vitez.

Acute eczema was confirmed and a proper regime of ointment prescribed. The medicines have yet to be obtained, but that will happen very soon. So the prognosis is good. Vanja's mother is a very relieved young lady, and I, too, will confess to a sense of satisfaction that Feed the Children has played no small part in putting Vanja on the road to recovery.

It was also on that Sunday morning that another young lady called Branpica Vosic came for help. An attractive, fair-haired 23-year-old, she had been a diabetic for eight years and now had only two weeks supply of insulin left. All stocks of insulin in the besieged Croat pocket of Vitez had expired long ago. Without insulin she faced certain death in a little over two weeks. A fate she shared with 100 other diabetics in this area.

Again it was a case of badger, cajole, wheedle, and eventually Medecin du Monde, the French aid agency, came to the rescue. Vitez hospital was visited, assessed for need, and given emergency supplies to tide them over. I was able to hand to Branpica sufficient insulin for 100 days, and once again felt that deep satisfaction that Feed the Children has averted the very real prospect of death for an innocent victim of the terrible war.

LIFE IN VITEZ
For those who have not been there
by KIM RANDALL IN VITEZ, 22 JANUARY 1994

It's very hard to imagine life in Vitez unless you have actually stayed there for some time. Certainly the impression that I had created in my mind's eye was very different from the reality. Vitez is not a pretty place in the English sense. Yet it lies in the Lasva Valley surrounded by gentle mountains which give it a certain rural beauty that compensates for its lack of architectural beauty. There are little pockets of excellence to be found if you take the time, like the parental home of our former interpreter, Tanya. It nestles alone, high in the cleft of three small intersecting hills. To the north the road that runs along the river to Zenica is stunning, even in winter, and, in your imagination, it would be easy to think you were in Wales or Scotland, or somewhere similar. I cannot wait to see it in springtime.

Yet nearly everywhere, this beauty is scarred by the destruction of people's homes. You become almost oblivious to it after a while, yet so much pointless and often random destruction hides sad and painful stories. One attractive wooden house lies on the side of a nearby hill. Until recently it was full of people living there. Now the fighting has badly damaged the building, and only the washing that still hangs across the upstairs balcony remains in memory of those people. Of course this story is the same for thousands across Bosnia and Croatia, and for people like you and me it is only when you see it with your own yes, experience the confrontation with your own mixture of feelings, that you can begin to understand a little of the pain and suffering.

I am always being asked what the people in England really think, why Europe just stands by weakly and lets this happen. I have to admit that few English people even know where Bosnia or Croatia are. That few understand what is happening over there, Bosnia being just another slot in the TV news; taking its place in the litany of stories of starvation and violence in other countries. Further, that after years of shock-horror news, people just become numb and not interested. Essentially in the rich West, we have become too self-ish to care until something directly affects us. Therefore we can only start to imagine this stark reality if we try to look from behind the eyes of those desperate and frightened people in order to see and feel what they see and feel.

Try to imagine the village or town you live in attacked by people from a nearby town or village, your home burnt by them, maybe people you know coming in and murdering members of your family and looting your possessions. In a small space of time everything you have worked for and built up is destroyed. From enjoying a good and comfortable standard of living you now have to suffer the indignity of begging for help, for food and clothing, toothpaste and toilet paper. Try to imagine, really imagine, how you would feel to have no water, no electricity, no postal system, no normal phone system, little possibility of communication with people you love and care about. (Even we become a little desperate and excited when our mail comes in.)

Of course it's hard for you to imagine, because it seems so impossible or unlikely in, say, Reading or Newbury or Harrogate. But then you must remind yourself that the people in Sarajevo, Tuzla or Vitez would have said that it was impossible for them three years ago. The shock of their rude awakening will leave scars in their souls for years. We have so much to learn from these people, from those whose spirit manages to soar above it all. For me, it is the children in all their innocence who teach us to be strong, to be less selfish. They are old before their time over here, for responsibility is thrust upon them early, and so many of them rise to the task with smiling faces and willing hands.

I will never forget sitting in the street, in the darkness, waiting for a truck to return that was long over-due. There had been a lot of fighting that day, and the sound of gunfire and occasional shelling was all around. Several of the local children sensed my anxiety and came and sat with me. One little girl went and got my guitar, and we all sat playing songs together in the darkness until the lorry returned. It was a most beautiful hour.

The children are our future, and we must guide them well with kindness and care. There are times when it makes one feel privileged to be here, and sometimes it compensates for all the stress, the endless mud and dampness, and the deprivation which one has to learn to tolerate.

I am proud of what Feed the Children has done for so many in Bosnia, but none of us, either here or in Reading, should become consumed by our own importance, for the reality is that what we actually achieve is only a drop in the ocean compared with what is needed. The reality is that we probably need small continuous teams of good people to make new inroads up here, and for anyone working here for long, the reality is that seen or unseen, the scars will remain with us for ever.

SEVEN DAYS
in Bosnia and Croatia

REPORT BY STEPHEN BIRD, MEDIA LIAISON OFFICER
FEED THE CHILDREN (EUROPE), JANUARY 1994

The area of Vitez, centred in the twenty-mile Lasva Valley of central Bosnia, is where some of the worst fighting and atrocities of the current conflict have occurred. I travelled there recently to see at first hand the work of Feed the Children.

An agreement to allow the free flow of UN humanitarian aid convoys throughout the country had earlier been undertaken by all three Bosnian factions and meant that, in theory, UN convoys should be allowed to get through.

According to the UNHCR, 1.2 million people in central Bosnia, 80 per cent of the region's population, need help to survive the winter. But in November only 10 per cent of the required supplies got through; in December just 17.9 per cent. Yet in spite of all the difficulties, Feed the Children teams in Vitez delivered more aid to mothers and children in the area than ever before.

DAY 1 — Zagreb, former Yugoslavia's most sophisticated metropolis, is about two hours' flight from Heathrow on Croatia Airlines. One of the first things you notice is the boarded-up welcome desk. Not a good sign for a country that relies heavily on tourism. The shuttle flight took me to the port of Split. Total distance/travelling time from London, roughly 1,600 km/three hours. By contrast, the Convoy that left besieged Sarajevo for Split just after Christmas with 1,000 Serbs, Croats and Muslims, a journey of roughly 160 km, took five days.

Croatia is a beautiful maritime country. Its Adriatic coast is nearly 6,400 km long. The climate is Mediterranean and widely renowned for its sunshine. The Feed the Children Aid Supply Centre is close to Split airport and convenient for the local Customs office.

The contrast between this part of Croatia and Bosnia-Hercegovina is extraordinary. In Split people go about their workaday life and everything appears normal. Although you may hear distant gunfire, 'Probably shooting rabbits' says cynics, the only visible signs of conflict are a few bullet holes in the airport control tower. Yet a few kilometres up the road, a dreadful civil war is being waged.

The day I landed, former US first lady Barbara Bush, as a US ambassador at large for humanitarian matters, arrived to tour refugee camps and visit a hospital in Split.

DAY 2 — HQ BRITFOR Daily Brief for UNHCR and NGOs (Non-governmental Organizations). Captain Liz Whichelo summarized the general political, humanitarian and security situation. Central Bosnia was reported relatively calm, but there had been limited shelling and small arms fire in Gornji Vakuf. In Vitez there had been a decrease in mortar and artillery fire. Mortar impacts in the centre of Vitez had landed near the huge ammunition factory. The route would be open the next day.

The Lava Hotel, on the seafront of Split, is home for 1,000 refugees from Bosnia. Among them more than 450 children. Here I met a group of teachers who, with aid from Feed the Children and other NGOs, were aiming to establish a primary school. In response to urgent appeals, Feed the Children had provided books, pencils, blackboards and chalk.

On the other side of Split I visited a cement factory where another school was being set up for an estimated 150 children. There is an obvious need at both places for educational aid.

DAY 3 — 'The convoy is stuck until the road has been cleared,' explained a helpful UNPROFOR officer. So began a five-hour delay, one of many encountered along the narrow, serpentine and often precipitous mountain road from Split to Vitez. Outside Prozor, a fuel tanker had gone off the road. There was little to do but wait.

The road, a remarkable piece of engineering, is the only main road from the coast inland and is the lifeline of aid to central Bosnia. Most of the territory of this part of the Balkans consists of mountains and plateaux. There are 144 peaks exceeding 1,950 metres in former Yugoslavia. Much of the route is through dense forests that cover more than a third of the mountainous country.

Checkpoints, official and unofficial, the weather, breakdowns and unscheduled stops, meant that the 240 km trip from Feed the Children's warehouse in

Split, to their forward supply centre in Vitez, took thirty hours instead of the estimated four.

In November a Danish lorry driver had been shot dead, apparently by government forces, and the convoy turned back. UN Aid convoys had been stopped for nearly a month.

The delay outside Prozor meant an overnight stay in the UN base at Gornji Vakuf, on the front line between Croatia and Muslim forces. Tracer bullets occasionally lit up the sky. Automatic gun fire, joined by the spasmodic whumph of mortars, echoed around the hills. Gornji Vakuf, where barely a building remains undamaged, is still home to 3,000 Muslims. A monumental thunder storm gave added drama to the bangs and flashes of the sporadic gunfire.

DAY 4 — Dawn revealed the extent of the army's presence. Dozens of tanks and armoured vehicles, road building and maintenance equipment, tractors and back hoes, Land Rovers and personnel carriers, all painted white, each vehicle carrying the familiar UN logo.

A hiss followed by a dull thud into the ground somewhere behind reminded me of the need for protective clothing. 'Incoming round. No trouble,' remarked a soldier.

The UNPROFOR convoy eventually moved off at 11.30. Half an hour later in dense woodland high in the mountains it stopped again. One of the leading vehicles had broken down. In an Alpine landscape of pines, jagged mountains and picturesque lakes, this was BonBon Alley, the nickname given by troops to a stretch of road where Muslim children swarm around convoys demanding sweets. Suddenly, dozens of children appeared as if from nowhere. Lurking a few yards into the woods could be seen shadowy figures — armed militia, perhaps? It was no place for a stroll.

The convoy started and stopped again and again. At one point a child was begging sweets from a troop carrier. Someone had given him a sandwich that he

213

concealed with one hand behind his back. Four older children ran up behind him, snatched his sandwich, divided it between them, and ran off. So it goes in central Bosnia.

DAY 5 — I accompanied a delivery of aid to the besieged town of Travnik, birthplace of Ivo Andvic, winner of the Nobel Literature prize. Nestled in a valley at the foot of Mount Vlasic, it is a sleepy, predominantly Muslim village once ruled by Turks.

In the no man's land that lies between checkpoints outside Vitez and Travnik, I ducked instinctively when a rife shot startled me as the truck passed through the minefield and barricades.

Because Feed the Children seems to have been accepted by all sides in this tragic conflict, it has earned the respect of the British UN forces. It also means that Feed the Children drivers can deliver aid to where it is most needed, unhindered by the warring factions.

Eventually, next to the 400-year-old mosque of Hadji Alis Beg, we unloaded a lorry load of baby food. Something like 10,000 babies and infants in the area rely on Feed the Children supplies.

Next I went to deliver more baby food to Vitez and the outlying villages of Busovaca, Nova Bila and Novi Travnik. The villages bear stark witness to the fratricidal strife that has plagued the communities. Many of the homes are burnt-out shells. Most buildings have been peppered with bullets and shrapnel. The apartment blocks have boarded-up windows and the streets are littered with broken glass and debris. The acrid smell of burnt buildings still hangs in the air. What nightmares had been experienced here do not bear thinking about.

What was extraordinary was that at first glance some of the communities give the impression of having been abandoned. Look closer and you notice smoke from one or two chimneys and washing hung out to dry. Children appear as from nowhere and help to unload the food and medical supplies.

Busovaca is next to Stari Vitez, a Muslim community blockaded by its Croatian neighbours since June, and where precious little aid get through at all — but some does . . . Pantechnicons barricade the roads leading into and out of the place. 'TNT High Explosive' crudely written on their side warns off would-be intruders. People say the only things coming in and out of Sari Vitez are bullets.

That night the rifle fire and mortar bombardment in the areas surrounding Vitez intensified. A large military helicopter landed in a quarry behind my temporary quarters. Later I learned the UN-declared no-fly zone had been broken on no fewer than 300 occasions in the first month it had been in place.

DAY 6 — Packed and ready to go at 7.30am. The bad news was, no escort. The good news was, a two-man team from Scot Aid were headed in the same direction. So, two vehicles being company where one comprised a target, we decided to make a run for it. With quick farewells we headed south.

Typically, a few kilometres down the road we met up with an unscheduled UN convoy, passing as we did a relief convoy headed in the opposite direction. Before long we reached the checkpoint outside Gornji Vakuf, where we were stopped by British soldiers and asked to wait for an escort, a Warrior armoured fighting vehicle of the Coldstream Guards UN Battalion.

While we waited, a young Bosnian soldier from the checkpoint brought a freshly-cooked local cheese delicacy in a large flan dish for us Brits to share. He stopped for a coffee and cigarette and, although the conversation was limited, seemed an agreeable young chap. A week later at this same spot a British APC was hijacked and although the soldiers were unharmed, their weapons had been taken and their vehicle burnt.

The journey back through the town of Gornji Vakuf can be even more intimidating in daylight. So it was with relief we eventually tucked in behind our Warrior escort. It was comforting when its twin hatches slammed shut and its gun began tracking known sniper locations.

The remainder of the journey into Split was uneventful and I arrived back at my hotel mid-afternoon. The journey had taken about eight hours, but had included a scheduled stop at Tomislavgrad, the UNPROFOR base, for a meeting with the British army.

CONCLUSION — I had been in Vitez for little more than a day. I had helped deliver six lorry loads of much needed aid directly into the hands of the suffering children. In Split I had helped load and unload five pantechnicons that had made the journey. I had also delivered aid to the children of some of the thousands of dispossessed who had escaped, or been driven, from the living nightmare that is central Bosnia.

In spite of all the difficulties facing aid agencies in this troubled country, the Feed the Children team struggles determinedly on, regularly delivering baby food, medical supplies and a lot of goodwill, direct to thousands of the helpless victims of the fighting.

Feed the Children teams in Split and Vitez work non-stop in this humanitarian effort. During the two weeks before Christmas in Vitez, Feed the Children delivered direct over 100 tonnes of UK aid. Since last October nearly £1.4 million worth of aid was delivered, an average of four 20-tonne truck loads a week, twice the amount of the previous quarter.

As for the future, it remains to be seen whether the delicately balanced co-operation between Feed the Children/UN drivers and the warring factions continues. What is certain is that unless the food and emergency supplies continue, people will starve.

CANDLES OF HOPE — Just before my arrival in Vitez the Coldstream Guards presented Feed the Children with a cheque for DM 3,000. Money contributed by men of The Cheshire, The Prince of Wales, and the Coldstream Guards Regiments. The money will buy crystals to make candles using special machines, obtained through 'Children in Crisis'. Enough to make 15,000 candles, many of which will be delivered by the Guardsmen who contributed some of their hard-earned pay.

At Christmas, before the war, hundreds of people from all around used to light candles and gather in descending tiers beneath a pretty hill top church behind the village. 'For miles around it was a beacon like one enormous Christmas tree,' explained Zeljo, our interpreter. It would be wonderful to think our candles could be used there next Christmas.

TRAVNIK
The Silent Children

by DAVID H. W. GRUBB
EXECUTIVE DIRECTOR, FEED THE CHILDREN (EUROPE)

In Travnik the maternity hospital has become a maternity hostel. The rooms are normally heated. Warm clothes are available. Milk and baby food are scarce. The nursing staff are attentive and positive, and deeply concerned.

Groups of women sit on the carpeted floor, the youngest children and babies with them. Some knit, most are totally silent. These women do not weep and the children do not play. There are no obvious signs of death or of food shortages or of sickness. But many of the babies have chest infections and very often the woman seated with the baby is not the mother but a

217

friend from the same village. The mother is dead or in a camp, and nothing is what it initially seems. Again, their sitting together is an expression of group relief, a mourning ritual, a form of sharing and communicating. These women are willing to have their photos taken. They are aware of media attention. They give names and ages of their children to journalists and aid workers. They will even smile for the camera.

Sitting down with them, asking about husbands and sons, asking about where they lived and how they had to leave, one enters another world. Trauma, terror, isolation; whatever word one chooses to use, these are the women and children and babies who have been terribly injured and yet have survived. They have no idea of what tomorrow may bring. Their certainties and hopes have been stripped away. They are hollow people and although there is care and evidence of nursing skill in this hospital, it is simply too early for hope.

In this same town the gymnasiums and schools have become hostels and there is a mortar attack every day. The hills surrounding the town no longer appear picturesque. They have become part of the technology of war. In crudely-constructed wooden beds or on mattresses, the refugees sleep or sit out the long days, wrestling with the dreams that must come. Again the children do not play, and nobody has the energy to organize recreation or lessons. This is surprising because there are teachers and other professional people here. Is it because they fear that to establish more order would be perceived as a sort of acceptance, an agreement to stay here, a signal not of organization but resignation? Have, therefore, skill and education, and also determination been killed?

The central heating system in the main gym no longer works. There have only been four bitterly cold days this winter. Log fires pump out smoke and stench and this itself can lead to bronchial problems. Because of fear of shelling, the refugees take little exercise, clinging to the small space that is the only thing they can call their own; a tiny island of retreat and dreams. And the children, what do they do here? A few run about with home-made toys, and wait for the aid workers to hand out some chocolate bars. There is nothing else for them. Apparently they have stopped asking questions about fathers and brothers. But what are they doing with the images and sounds, and what do they remember of their last sight of home?

There is little discipline in these hostels. There is little scolding. There is no way to spoil these children. So they also must feel the inner cold, experience the cycle of loss.

It is the lack of noise and laughter that most chills the onlooker.

END OF 11-MONTH SIEGE AT THE STARI VITEZ ENCLAVE

by MALCOLM TURNER
STARI BILA, CENTRAL BOSNIA, MARCH 1994

Today was a milestone for the team in Vitez, and particularly for the team leader, Jim Stuart. After eleven months of bitter fighting the Muslim enclave of Stari Vitez was at last allowed access to aid, the ceasefire holding and even strengthening. So with some excitement and not a little apprehension Jim and I set off in the Feed the Children Toyota Land-Cruiser laden with food and toiletries. Excitement because over the months the place had become a *cause célèbre*, particularly for Jim who was the longest-serving team member and in all of seven months in Central Bosnia he could not enter there; and apprehension because of the anticipation that we would be exposed to scenes of appalling deprivation.

The approach to the checkpoint does nothing to

dispel such feelings. UNPROFOR had replaced the old barricades of logs and old trucks with a chicane of purpose-built defences of a type that is a familiar sight around military installations in this country. Just beyond the checkpoint could be seen once beautiful houses ruined by artillery and blackened by fire. The scene at the checkpoint was one that would be strange to English eyes. The gap through which the vehicles have to pass was crowded with soldiers, some wearing the blue berets of the peace-keeping force, some in the uniform and insignia of the BiH, and the remainder in that of the HVO. Tucked just inside the barrier, a Warrior tank sat with engines idling, the door of the crew compartment wide open and the turret angled so that its 30mm gun pointed neutrally along the No Man's Land between the former factions.

We stopped the car and submitted to the interrogations which were oddly conducted with an absence of tension. But then there was a problem. The HVO said they had not been informed of our intention to enter Stari Vitez and they needed clearance from higher authority. We were made to wait.

Waiting for forty minutes before a potentially unpleasant task does nothing to calm the nerves, and patience is sorely tested. Only the desultory chat with the soldiers of the Coldstream Guards kept the jitters under control. Eventually Jim, who had shown remarkable restraint to this point, made his way to the HVO police station half a kilometre away and returned with permission to proceed. We got into the car and slowly rounded the barricades.

The first two hundred metres revealed horrendous scenes of devastation. Houses, once beautiful, reduced to burnt-out shells, their roofs gone and open to the sky. Rubble littered the road so that Jim, as he drove, had to pick his way carefully through the shards of broken glass and tiles. Looking at these scenes, I tried to picture what it had been like to undergo the barrage that had laid these homes to waste. Try as I might, I could not fix in my mind images so brutal that they would match the damage I could see around me.

Then it wasn't quite so bad. Less damage was evident as we drove deeper into the enclave, although here was still the detritus of armed conflict. The houses were protected by timber leant against the walls so that the windows should not be shattered by a blast.

It was here that we located the police station, the point to which we had been directed. As we got out of the car we were met by a woman, painfully thin by nature's design and only a little by denial, who spoke to us volubly in Serb-Croat.

We asked, 'Do you speak English?'

'A little,' she responded, but as we tried to converse it was obvious that we had exhausted her capability and we had to wait for a young girl to be fetched who could speak usable English.

While we stood a crowd began to gather around us — a familiar enough occurrence, but here there was a difference. They stood quietly, almost sullenly. There was none of the clamour that greeted us in other places. I searched their faces for the evidence of the effects of siege and the evidence was there; simply in the quietness of their demeanour.

After a while the girl was found and brought to us. She introduced herself as Kanita Muminovic, a small, exuberant 16-year-old with shoulder-length hair and a ready smile. She greeted us effusively.

We followed her and the thin woman to a nearby house. Again I felt a surge of anger that such lovely houses should be so diminished in facility. The inside of the house was well furnished but cold and darkened by the timber that covered the windows.

The woman and the girl worked for an Islamic charitable organization known as Merhamet, and they showed us records that they kept of the people of Stari Vitez. One thousand one hundred people lived in an area no bigger than five football pitches. One hundred had died. Two hundred and forty were children below the age of 15.

We were told of the man who had been visiting a friend in the area when war broke out and the barricades went up before he could return to his home just fifty metres away. For almost a year he could only shout to his wife but could not go to see her. Another man spent that time with his grandmother because he, too, was trapped behind the barricades, unable to return to his family a few short metres away.

When the meeting was over, we unloaded our aid and saw it safely into a store for later distribution. It was little enough but it was the first of a regular supply — a supply which will begin to put the occupants of Stari Vitez back on the road to a normal life. Slowly, we drove back along the road to the checkpoint.

I often wonder how native Bosnians view us with our freedom to cross lines of confrontation while they are trapped behind serpentine frontlines. At Stari Vitez, where from a high point the limits of their world can easily be seen no more than a few metres away. I reflected that any sense of envy they may have of us must be more acutely felt.

But the signs are encouraging. There is a ceasefire which may lead to peace and soon, with any luck, the barricades will disappear and become a thing of the past. Then, for us, our work will begin. Two hundred and forty children need our help and it will be months, even years, before the effects of war can be eradicated. Until they are, we will keep going back to Stari Vitez.

'THE WAR THAT WILL NOT GO AWAY'

Jerko Vrtar, 12 years

Field trip to Croatia and Bosnia
May 1994

by DAVID H. W. GRUBB
EXECUTIVE DIRECTOR, FEED THE CHILDREN (EUROPE)

RETURNING TO SPLIT. Flying into Zagreb; warm rain, passport control, security check, fifty minutes spent between the London/Zagreb flight and the Zagreb/Split flight; occupying the same seat on the same aircraft after all this delay. Flying over the thousand islands to sunlit Split. The airport could be at Rhodes, the white UN vehicles signalling the fact that we are near to a war zone. The café and restaurant signs, the beaches, the hotels, don't attract tourists any more. On the first night at dinner we are hosted by Croatians who have known of our work from the first days, who wish to say

223

'thank you' with Croatian food and wine. We also want to celebrate the work achieved, the fact that we believe we can do even more.

DAY OF THE PIGS. Having checked out of the warehouse after a night of huge winds and little sleep, we head off down the Dalmatian coast to visit a so-called 'Children's Village' near to Makarska. Before leaving Split a small soft-sided lorry is holding us up, slowing us down, and suddenly a small pig falls out onto the road. Shocked, winded, amazed, it somehow gets up and makes it to the kerb. Within seconds (before we ham it up with piggy jokes) a second pig slips from the lorry and hits the road, and stays there as we deftly avoid it. Catching up with the vehicle isn't easy, but we finally force it to a halt and, while the rest of the cargo grunts away, we explain things to the driver and his mate, and discover a shifted floor plank at the rear of the vehicle. We drive on, piggy jokes still trotting out.

An hour later and having passed extraordinarily beautiful harbours, villages and marinas, we drive into the 'Children's Village' set up with support from the Queen of Sweden in the 1930s on a fee-paying basis, offering hospitalization for asthmatic children. There are 300 people here now; about eighty children and thirty geriatrics, the rest refugees/displaced adults. We are here to see if there is anything Feed the Children can do. It becomes clear that there is immense uncertainty in the mind of the director, there is uncertainty re. the funding, and even the current and future purpose of the place. The director is fighting to retain the specialist staff. The refugees/displaced people are taking up valuable space. He feels they must be moved on. He is not happy to be in charge of a refugee centre, to run a hostel instead of a hospital, a specialist sanatorium set in a beautiful place by the sea. He is fighting to recreate the dream place in his head.

We are shown over the buildings where the aged are kept. Small, fragile, very old relics of Croatia and

Bosnia stare back at us, allow us to take photographs, hold our hands. In winter it must be incredibly cold here. Today these ancient souls inhabit their very last holiday camp.

Returning to Split I notice places where a year ago there were refugee camps, thousands of people existing beneath canvas. Now they live in the hotels, or in Slovenia, or they have gone abroad, or they are dead.

We visit a refugee camp that I had been to three times before. On each visit I have been impressed by the way the small rooms and corridors are kept. It is a temporary village where the passageways are swept almost every hour. Rooms where five or six live together, hugging their culture and sanity. They dream of places elsewhere, in Srebrenica and Mostar and Sarajevo. People who float between dreams and desires, tidying up the present reality, keeping the horror and dust at bay. The children attend school each day at the Hotel Lav, a few miles away. Many of the older women wear national dress. The younger men and women are missing. Not like Schindler's List, not a place of pain on a brilliantly warm and sunny day. But as on all my previous visits here, not a real place; a waiting place, people waiting to become whole again.

We visit a school set up in a factory nearby. The teachers are determined to get books, pencils, paper, a sense of identity and purpose. The desks, the children studying, the teachers, all give a good and positive image, but it is the pictures on the walls that signify the most. The children's drawings clearly show how the horrors of war have impacted upon them.

Back at the warehouse we see another truck loaded up. Tomorrow we depart at 6am for Bosnia, for the war.

DAY OF THE MOUNTAIN ROADS. The nature of the journey from Vitez to Split depends entirely on the roads created by the military; carved out, pushed through, punched across the mountain terrain where once there was a lane, a track, nothing.

225

The roads get wider, the surfaces are improved. There are even road signs created out of oil drums marking out the miles. These roads have changed dramatically in the last twelve months. What was essentially military and aid agency traffic has become commercial trucks, individual aid vehicles, even coaches and cars. The few convoys a day have become giant convoys, log jams of lorries, queues on the still perilous mountain top corners. Abandoned wrecks are all too evident. It is this upturn in traffic that represents the gradual transformation from war to the slow progress of a truce.

It is a brilliantly bright day. Dust from the road swirls up. We pass through what were previously checkpoints, now little bits of history. The danger currently is in negotiating the road. There are some crazy drivers up here.

One is constantly aware that without the roadway little aid would ever have got in. This is not merely a superb example of British engineering and determination, but a strategy for peace for the people who did get the aid and were fed and supplied. In winter it is a dramatic terrain, often swept by huge winds. Today is a clear spring day. The blossom in farm gardens and in hamlets hangs like bunting and lilac flames in most cottage doorways. The roadway is now being severely tested by commercial vehicles, unsuitable vehicles, bad driving. In places the surface is rapidly deteriorating. This increase in commercial vehicles heralds a peaceful future but one wonders who will maintain the roads when the army has left.

In early May this countryside can be amazing. The people appear to spend all day in their gardens, or working in fields. We pass scenes which remind us of Austria. Three men work a horse-drawn plough. A few small shops tentatively begin to trade. Each passing day, lorries bring purpose and hope; green tufts of trust.

The checkpoints have all but gone. The young

soldiers we used to see who were half starved and very aggressive are no longer in evidence. The terror and coldness has moved away from this part of Bosnia. And then we enter Gornji Vakuf.

FRAIL PEACE AT GORNJI VAKUF. A truce is hardly a peace. At Gornji Vakuf it is even frailer. It means that the barrel bombs no longer roll down the hillside, crushing all before them until they explode, shattering  entire streets. It means that snipers have ceased their deadly work and the people are able to walk in the street, and begin to come to terms with the fact that so many have apparently survived. But there are so many other things that they are unable to come to terms with.

On each visit to Bosnia this is where the slaughter was most revealing, the squalor of neighbour hacking at neighbour was most evident. It is a small place. One could not drive through it without a military escort. Bombardment took place daily, deliberate and devastating.

Now there is a sort of truce; but what can be done with it? Children play at war in the rubble. UN soldiers have become symbols of care and concern. The lines between the Muslims and the Croats are still drawn out. This is a divided town and it may be for decades unless there is a massive upsurge of spirit of reconciliation. Such reconciliation is not likely to come from the mosque or the church. Stories of atrocities, dead bodies, ghosts, the rubble, the architecture of hate, all bar the way. What is most likely to reconcile, perhaps, in the play groups and the schools, the places shared by women and children, is a recognition of futility.

This is a lost, lost town. There were never likely to

be any winners. Everyone has lost. Two of the children
playing by the UN Warrior are twenty yards from their
home. Their parents were killed there. Now grandparents must take up again the caring role. Their home
is a rubble pile above a cellar. The hospital near the
bridge where the first British soldier was slain looks
more like a deserted warehouse. The doctors and
nurses are there; they wear white coats, they begin to
clean up the mess. The roof is in need of major repair.
This hospital has been the target of countless attacks
and now supplies of medicines, equipment, everything
a hospital needs, are most urgently required.

Feed the Children hands over an ambulance to the
Hospital director and a municipal chief. A slightly
awkward ceremony takes place; hands are shaken,
papers signed, thanks expressed. This takes place outside the hospital, in brilliant sunshine, near to the
place called Barrel Bomb Alley. The fact that we can
stand here and talk is itself worth celebration. The
ambulance is possibly the most useful gift we can provide at this stage. It means children can be picked up
from the neighbouring villages and hamlets as well as
the towns, and not left in this hospital if their needs
exceed the expertise or medicines. It puts Gornji Vakuf
on the map as a centre that cares. It begins to resurrect
a sense of opportunity and confidence. This is
essential.

We see the buffer lines, the remaining markers of
division. We sense the continuing tensions created by
uncertainty. One mistake, one further act of vengeance
and hatred could set these civilians off again. We are
invited by the municipal chief to have some lunch at
the café in the town centre. We accept. It gives us time
for discussion. It gives the director and the municipal
chief a chance to take up the mantle of respectability
and it offers an opportunity to hear something about
their uncertainty and fragile hopes. As always, the
atrocity stories have to be detailed as if we have no
awareness of the terrible centre of this conflict. The

man mainly responsible for the barrel bombs; who is he, where is he, how could he kill so many defenceless people? Apparently his wife and children were caught and crucified and then slit open. Between our horror, revulsion and compassion, we can so easily see these actions in our minds. Every ruined building and slogan and pile of rubble shrieks out terrible demons at Gornji Vakuf. The terror is carried by every survivor. It is so young this truce; talk of lasting peace is still a broken whisper.

Between our elation, the handshakes, the smiles, we feel uneasy still. We try to think of what it would be like to return perhaps as tourists in ten years' time. This is a very old town. Many hundreds of aid trucks will continue to cross the bridge. Gornji Vakuf is at a strategic position for development but first it has to come to terms with what has happened and begin to build trust, confidence. As the 'cabbage trucks' (commercial lorries) roll in, one wonders what they carry,  the price of it, and whether there are also concealed arms on board. Ironies abound. The British army created these roads from tracks to enable the aid programme. Now the 'cabbages' are wrecking the road surface and there is a threat that all vehicles over 5 tonnes will have to pay DM 100 each. A road tax, a toll, not to benefit the road makers and the maintenance crews, but armies who retain all the tension and fears.

In Gornji Vakuf Feed the Children will plan to supply civilians at the hospital, the schools and the play groups, helping build for peace. As we drive off on the road to Vitez we experience the extremes of relief and continuing concern. How do these people begin to build the foundations of trust? How do these children begin to learn to play peacefully again? The Croatian word for 'war' is 'rat' and the stench of that vermin is everywhere.

THE GHOSTLY RUINS OF VITEZ. Around the town of Vitez the hills no longer hide snipers, but in recent days mosques and a petrol station have been torched. We pass two burnt-out buses and see where trenches existed in the small fields. The ghostly ruins of torched houses create a mosaic of madness. We pass the house where several hundred bodies were found. Even the dogs were shot. Each shell of a house conjures up images of horror where the young and old were told to hate each other. Here at Vitez burnt-out garages, fallen minarets, hills of debris and flame stains create a quilt of guilt and insane compulsion. Some took to killing and became soldiers of hatred. Some took to arms out of red-hot revenge. And some killed because they were so terrified, hacking back at real and imagined neighbours who had become murderers in their minds.

The litter of war lies everywhere, strewn in the streets and fields and also by the riverside. Rags catch on the sticks and shrubs, and from a distance look like the rags placed at holy wells. One's mind creates the images of the people who drowned. The fields of Vitez became killing fields and it is impossible to consider that the adults will ever totally erase such terrors from their minds.

TRAVNIK SURROUNDED BY GUNS. Arriving at Travnik we visit once again the hostel for refugees and displaced people. In airless rooms, squatting on mattresses, gypsies and teachers, shopkeepers and accountants survive one day at a time. They wait for letters, messages, sightings of their loved ones. The town is still attacked several times each day and it may yet become a slaughter house like Gorazde because it is mainly Muslim. The gun installations sit on the mountain top for all to see. People out walking live within the expectation that any moment could be their last. We visit the Centre for Women and Babies and see the new burial plot for the Muslim dead. This city of considerable beauty and immense history has been reduced to a cowering camp for those who have nowhere else to go.

 I recognize people I first saw here over two years ago. In the hostel I see their only belongings hanging on nails from the walls. They live on rumours. They share scraps of stories. They constantly clean the toilets and corridors. They believe in a future but don't know to whom it will belong.

THE JOURNEY TO TUZLA. We travel on metal roads, on tracks, on rock, on mud to get to Tuzla from Vitez. At Zenica we see Paul Goodalls' memorial by the river where he died. Zenica is always busy. The aid convoys create an atmosphere of endeavour and purpose, but the tension cannot be hidden. Zenica is hot with plots and politics.

We pass cottages that could be in Devonshire and valleys reminiscent of Wales, trashed villages and even castles. We are near to the front-line. At Vares and Kladanj soldiers, horse-drawn carts, scenes from normal life clash with burnt-out buildings, ruined mosques, orchards and rivers and children keeping a watch on the passing aid trucks whose drivers might throw out chocolate bars and sweets and cigarettes. They stand on hairpin bends and risk everything. And Tuzla itself has become an intricate system of allotments. They are literally digging for victory here, propagating for peace, seeding for the future. It is incredibly impressive.

TUZLA'S SUSTAINING ALLOTMENTS. We meet other aid agencies at Tuzla and discuss needs at the UNHCR building and feel that progress is possible so long as the war does not return. But it probably will, either directly or because the Muslim community feel compelled to assist their brothers and sisters in Brcko when the Serbs decide to widen the corridor. There is no reason whatsoever to doubt that this will happen at some time, and thousands will die horribly.

We spend the evening in the apartment of a family of four. They speak of their lives during the past two years. He has set up a small shop and café near the railway station. When the trains run again he may do well. She is a doctor. Their two daughters are a delight, responding to gifts and hugs and the fun of receiving foreign visitors and trying out their little bits of English.

The father was forced to join the army. He sees no end to the war. His wife knows they are comparatively well off and that any day this could all die. They serve us coffee and chicken and ham and bread and we eat very little. It is an honour to share their home for an evening. It is an honour to listen to their stories, however painful. This family is living in the present, making it work. There is nowhere for them to flee to. They have each other and will, if need be, die to save other similar families.

Late at night I look out from my bedroom at the allotments. There are still people at work there, small fires giving them light. At 5am the next morning I get up and they are at work again. This land, this earth may save them yet.

MOVING NORTH ALONG THE FRONT LINE. From Tuzla we work along the front line to Srebnica and Gradacac. Small-arms fire can be heard in the background. People are on the move. It is a warm day now and we need to make contact with relatives of friends.

The elderly couple who have sheltered in this village for over two years, unable to work and earn for much of that time, have barricaded their cottage, lived off their garden produce, and seen the village trashed. The noise and chaos of war continues a few kilometres away. They receive news of their daughter in Split and are able to talk to her using our Codan. Families meet by messages, letters, rumours; a telephone call or photograph is a luxury. Each day these people supply themselves with cold water, bread, cheese, coffee, soap, and when these things don't exist, count themselves lucky simply to be alive. They worry about the daughter in Split and the daughter who has gone abroad. They would like to see their grandchildren. Their wants and needs are unexceptional.

After visiting the hospital and delivering some supplies, we head back to Vitez. At 4pm we miss the UN convoys, the 'cabbage trucks', and the rain keeps the road dust down. People are working in gardens and fields in the rain. They don't miss any opportunity to plant and grow for the future.

MAGLAJ, BLOCKADED FOR NINE MONTHS. Reaching Maglaj, we enter a community that was blockaded for nine months. At first it is hard to find the town centre because of the massive damage. In a few streets it all looks so normal, but around the corner one finds gutted, ruined, trashed buildings. We find a school that has opened and visit the local Red Cross and note the large paper factory that has closed down. There is no energy. Machines have been wrecked. There are no raw materials. There is no way to pay the workers. Even if there was power and repaired machines and raw materials and pay for the workers, who would buy the product?

The children at the school are glad to get back to the order, conformity, security of lessons. They need pens and paper and other resources but for the moment simply being there is good. The schools offer trust, care and a future. Some of the schools need sandbagging and protection. The playgrounds are still vulnerable. In a war where civilians are targets these children are still at risk. As well as educational materials they need food. They need a regular small supply of aid boxes to take home.

IMAGES OF TESANJ. Leaving for Tesanj we drive

into the hills and again enter a world of ruin. We are surrounded by debris and destruction; one cannot keep the images of screaming people out of one's mind.

At the hospital we find that the children who were once patients have been sent home. The hospital is a main target. We see one mother and child too ill to be moved, and another extremely sick girl who needs a further operation. The hospital building is still heavily protected and soldiers with rifles are on duty. We deliver some aid and then head back for Vitez.

Our route is through ghost towns.

URGENT NEEDS AT PAZARIC. At the Psychiatric Hospital at Pazaric we see many of the patients we visited over two years ago. The hospital is now thankfully well supplied. I recall how it was the British army who first told us about this place when no aid came. They could do with five wheelchairs. They certainly have a need for shoes and clothes but for the moment their crisis is over. The toilets are clean. The dormitories are clean, although basic. In winter it must be very cold here, but the inmates are active and cheery, save for those in the smallest wards designed for the extremely handicapped. I had thought previously that they were well cared for, but I am less sure now. Had they slipped to the bottom of a huge pile? Do they get exercise; what physiotherapy do they receive? I do not see bedsores, there is no evidence of ill treatment or other abuse, there is no stench of urine and the sheets are dry, but why do they lie here all day? Their heads appear above the blankets, lost souls, mostly sleeping their lives away. They respond to our visit, the camera, our voices, but they need more than this. However, the nurses have not run away, have never deserted these poor people, and in Bosnia this is to be especially noted when the nurses have worked for so long beneath the Serbian guns. The cemetery in the hillside is bigger. The director is, I think, a dedicated man. What this place needs now is more than a truce, a real peace, space to develop caring skills.

MOSTAR, CITY OF LOST BEAUTY. We travel on via the Bijelco ferry to what remains of Mostar. We give a lift to a grandmother and her granddaughter who fled Mostar seven months ago. They look out with us at the total devastation as we approach this ancient city once famous for its architecture, bridge, river. It is as if Prague or Vienna or Bath had been ravaged. As always it amazes us how systematic the killing and destruction have been. The grandmother is caught between the delight of returning home, the cessation of shooting, and the horror of rubble, ruin, wreckage. There must be some places she simply cannot recognize.

We walk down to the site of the ancient bridge. The river has a special glacier hue. The current bridge is a rope and wire affair and as we walk across we are aware of the symbolism as well as the strategic importance of this river crossing.

The buildings on either side have been cut down, reduced, bombarded flat. When I was last here there was a coffee shop and a metalwork shop and a line of half-surviving buildings. All have gone. The only shape that remains is the shape of the river.

Children beg in Mostar, for pencils and biros and something to write on. As attempts are made to open the schools these children go begging for resources. They need to get back to words and numbers and they also need to express themselves. This is where our Education Aid programme can respond to specific needs.

As we take the road out of Mostar we look down on the city. One is silenced by the desolation. Poppies grow on the rubbish piles.

We have seen old men in the streets who must wonder whether they will ever live long enough to see a peace. We have seen soldiers, young men, made permanently deaf by the extreme noise of warfare. The bright sun and brilliant hue of the river does little to lighten our minds. The immense tragedy of Bosnia, so evident in villages and towns, appears magnified in Mostar simply because of its lost beauty, its ancient identity.

RETURNING TO ENGLAND WITH POPPIES. Flying back to Heathrow. Baggage soiled from 1,600km of travel. Poppies from Mostar pressed into the rear pages of the log book. Metaphors. Discover the business card of the Civic Chief in Gornji Vakuf. His name is Omar. Remember he made a joke about Omar Sharif. In my hand luggage fir cones from the so-called 'Children's Village'. Also letters from British soldiers to post to Germany. And a letter to a doctor from a sister in the Hotel Lav, Split, where over 1,000 refugees/displaced people still survive. Do they ever enjoy the sun, the beach, the sea, or is that still impossible?

In my bag a small parcel from Sister Juliana; a bone scrape sample for analysis in London and a letter of explanation. I return home with children's drawings and poppies and fir cones and a specimen from a child's bone.

MOSTAR
City of utter destruction

by JON SCOURSE
FEED THE CHILDREN CORPORATE LIAISON OFFICER, MAY 1994

Our journey continues under brilliant blue skies, towards Jablanica and then Mostar. The countryside is becoming much more rugged as we enter the Neretva Valley and follow it southwards. The valley soon turns into a gorge, with the road hugging the river. Lower down the river has been dammed for HEP schemes, so it becomes a brilliant azure blue lake. The road is good, but lower down the valley the Serbs have totally destroyed the bridges at Bijela. We have a choice: over the mountains on exposed and challenging road, or to take the UN ferry recently established. After advice from SPANBAT, we opt for the latter. We are lucky, thanks to some mild cheek from Gordon, to get onto the first ferry without a long wait. This is a most unusual contraption; pontoons have been linked together, and are pushed by two launches downstream. The journey takes about forty-five minutes, passing the blown up bridges to rejoin the road further downstream. The helmsmen are unable to see the way ahead, so a soldier is posted on top of the vehicles with flags to indicate the way ahead. While on board we are approached by several refugees to see if we can give them a lift into Mostar.

We empty the back of the Toyota and five pile in. At first their demeanour is excitement. They are returning to Mostar, having fled the town some nine months earlier to Jablanica. But as we proceed the extent of the devastation by the Serb forces — a scorched earth policy — silences them. This intensifies as we approach Mostar itself. They ask to be let out, and the look on their faces as they see this once beautiful town will haunt me.

We arrive at last in Mostar. There is no escape, no retreat to be found, from utter destruction. We pass what was once the railway station, with ruptured roof, no glass, and no life. Piles of rubble line the streets through which the Toyota has to twist its way with care. Whole buildings hang at crazy angles, one block of flats has ruptured in the middle, huge holes in houses. How could these people survive this? We pass what was once an attractive city park, shaded by palm trees with seats for tourists to relax in between sightseeing. Now every inch of this park is full of graves — makeshift graves with simple wooden Muslim headboards. It was the only place that could be used without the risk of snipers, but even here the once beautiful dome at the entrance has been toppled by shells.

People queue at standpipes. Cars are peppered with shrapnel. Is there anywhere in Mostar that is safe — only dark cellars for months on end. We park above the approach to the old arched bridge destroyed by Croat fire. In brilliant sunshine the azure blue of the Neretva river winds below, with the makeshift wire hawser bridge spanning where the old bridge was. It is easy to imagine how beautiful this city must have been, and I feel angry, really angry. We cross the bridge which swings unsteadily, and it is wise not to look down the 100-foot drop into the river below. What was once the thriving bazaar on the west bank is now empty, with the occasional man sitting on the pavement. Tudzman is mentioned as we pass, and it is clear that these Muslims are not reconciled to peace. Looking at the rape of Mostar, it is hard not to feel sympathetic to their feelings. One can see the suffering on their faces, and not for the first time I feel uncomfortable flippantly taking photographs. How do *they* feel after having no help from the international community for months on end, then, when peace breaks out, we descend into the town with our Nikons?

As we return some graffiti catches my eye. High above the river, in a damaged shelter, are the words 'DO NOT FORGET'. A young boy approaches me, not to beg for 'bon-bons', but asking for a pen or pencil, or even paper. This reinforces the need to satisfy their hunger to return to normality, and while the NGO community concentrates on food, Feed the Children can do so much in this area. As we return towards the outskirts of town, four BiH soldiers are walking in the street ahead. They fail to move out of our way, so Gordon toots the horn. Still no response — we toot again, and then a passing woman alerts them to our presence. They smile and wave, pointing at their ears, indicating deafness. The constant shelling and continuous defence of Mostar has made these young men deaf for life.

The road leaving Mostar passes above the ancient city, and we can look down on the extent of the destruction below. How anyone can survive the psychological trauma of the last two years and still hold out, says much for the determination of these proud people. The irony is that during the Second World War Mostar was able to survive through the support of the various communities for each other — Serbs helped Muslims, and Croats refused to fight Serb neighbours. As such it stood as a monument to peace.

Mostar needs enormous assistance, and I hope that somehow Feed the Children can find a role here.

And so we leave Bosnia. Once across the border normality returns and trashed houses are now the exception and not the rule. At Metkovic we cross the Neretva and head north to join the Adriatic coast. In an hour we have left behind one of the greatest war crimes of the late twentieth century, to find the tranquillity of the Dalmatian coast in the evening sunshine. Empty beaches beckon non-existent tourists, and the traffic is all painted white, bearing the letters UN.

And Shakespeare's words in Hamlet echo in my mind: 'When sorrows come, they come not as single spies, but in battalions.'

THE MEANING OF DAYLIGHT

Rat I Mir (War and Peace) Nataša, II, from Pula

Education Aid for Croatia and Bosnia

by DAVID H. W. GRUBB
EXECUTIVE DIRECTOR, FEED THE CHILDREN

In all my visits to Croatia and Bosnia at the height of
hostilities, I had been aware of children left alone to
their own devices. I had seen this near Split, in hostels
and refugee camps and in ruined villages. Life had
been so totally changed by bombardment and revenge
that normal activities such as recreation and education
had been abandoned. It was no longer safe for children
to gather. The schools had been deliberately targeted.
Education was a thing of the past and therefore too
close to ethnic identification. Schools could only
mean something if there was a belief in a future.
Therefore they were redundant. There was nothing to
teach with and there was nothing to teach about. For
refugees and displaced people to set up a classroom
was to signify acceptance of the current situation

which was to accept defeat, failure. Anyway, soon they would all be allowed to 'go home and take up the old life'. And in many places the children and teachers were too traumatized, too hurt, too punished to speak, to tell, to learn. It was more than their bodies that were broken.

In some places lessons did continue, mostly for the very young. In the Hotel Lav, near Split, there was a room set aside for lessons. Small pictures appeared on the walls. The nuns somehow supplied pencils and paper. But there were periods when even here, in what had been a beautiful coastal hotel, the huge shadow of pain and anger and uncertainty overpowered the creative urge to teach and learn.

In Croatia earlier on, and more recently in Bosnia, there have always been some children who could continue to write and draw and even write stories. In Mostar some classes continued to meet even in the worst months. What drove them was a stubborn refusal to let go, a massive sense of purpose, and for some no doubt there was nothing else to do. By candlelight, in basements, beneath rubble, within a city in chaos, learning still took place.

As the war continued we were aware of this. On visits to Travnik, Nova Bila, Vitez, Gornji Vakuf, we saw or heard of the fight to enable the mind to keep skills alive. And even early on there were the pictures. So many of these images were of homes which had lost everything that gave them meaning. The windows now appeared like wounds. The walls and roofs were only half there, cut away like the trees. The rubble piles contained wood, bricks, bodies, farm animals and pets. In many of the pictures bedrooms and church towers, bells and bombs, tanks and toys merged in madness.

One drawing by a young girl is entitled 'Our Home'. It shows a house but no longer a home. Its trust and wholeness have been bombed away. Another drawing shows in intricate detail the ancient bridge at Mostar; but we all know that the bridge is no longer there. How do we tell this child that her image has become history? In one picture even the fish in the ocean look like missiles and each house has the face of a weeping child staring from it.

Hundreds of such images have come out of the killing zones, but these child artists have been the lucky ones. They have had paper and pencils, crayons and even paints to put their feelings down, to tell their story, to identify. In hospital wards, cellars, camps, shelters, thousands have been plunged into an expressionless silence between the military onslaughts so loud that thousands of surviving soldiers have been made permanently deaf. In this silence the pain and defeat has cut into their souls past any expression. These children cannot remember what they saw and heard and had done to them. They cannot remember what they did. At this moment no word or shape or shade can tell us or inform them.

Children beg in Mostar and other places; for crayons and biros, something to write on. They need to express themselves in shapes, texts, colours. They need to find themselves again and write out, act out, draw the war and what it meant to them.

To survive now they need places of neutrality, security, peace, and these are only to be found in classrooms. They need space to stand up spiritually, and only the schools can offer this. They need to grip the pen and hold the ruler and carry out routines, sing and play. They need to run to and fro from the schools each day and know that they are safe and have a right to be there. To cross a bridge, walk down a street, enter a classroom is a proof of survival. And their teachers need such trust also.

The teachers have to pick up and begin again. The teachers have to believe in this classroom of hope and faith and nurture. The teachers, one by one, have to clear out the rubble and set to finding equipment and reintroducing order and purpose amid ruin, the shadows of guilt and revenge. These teachers have the entire future in their hands, and need skills beyond most of us. They need a bright sun and a brilliant hue of hope in their souls to lift the children up from the tragedy.

If these children don't find such classrooms and teachers and cannot fully play out their traumas and their stories, their identities will never be rediscovered. The huge denials of recent years will prevent their belief and acceptance of the current possibilities. The sounds of schoolroom and playground will never penetrate.

If these teachers are denied the impulse to create a future then all has been lost and recovery will take too many generations. The echoes of revenge, denial and hatred will sound on.

We who have delivered the life-saving, hope-giving aid in the last two years have to recognize that following supplementary feeding programmes, food for the mind is the current priority. In Bugojno, Gornji Vakuf, Travnik, Busovaca, Novi Bila, Vitez, Novi Travnik, Stari Vitez and Kakanj, we have 35,256 pupils aged between 7-15 years needing our help; what of the younger ones and what of those in other places? Our work has changed, this work is equally essential to make the meaning of peace a reality.

We have to respond to this need speedily, in Croatia and Bosnia, whatever the autumn and winter brings. We have to take educational aid into places like Maglaj, Tuzla and Gradacac as well. We need to get into Gorazde and Srebrenica and Brcko in time. Should there be a total reversal of the move towards peace, we will deliver this sort of aid to the children town by town, school by school.

This is another type of aid. It makes the first phase of aid more meaningful. It enhances our purpose to help the helpless and build up hope.

The letters and messages we receive from children and teachers in former Yugoslavia say it all.

'We are afraid we shall forget what the words

GAMES, SONGS, and DAYLIGHT, mean. We can't go to our school because it is badly damaged by shells. Our carefree childhood and school-days have gone together with the destruction of our school buildings.'
(From children in Novi Travnik)

We have to remember that in this war children and mothers were the targets day by day, and therefore schools, playgrounds and maternity wards in particular. This was a war on people.

We have now to return the games and songs, the resources to teach and learn, indeed the daylight and all that this should mean.

DELIVERING AID
IN A TOWN
UNDER FIRE

by PETER ANNEREAU
PROCUREMENT MANAGER, FEED THE CHILDREN,
31 OCTOBER 1994

The streets of Bugojno are empty, not a soul in sight. Windows boarded up, large tree trunks stacked against the sides of buildings.

The eerie silence is suddenly broken by the wailing of a siren. My colleagues drive straight to the British UNPROFOR camp where we are ushered into sand-bag covered shelters.

Minutes later we are under attack; Serb shells raining in all around.

Bosnia may have fallen out of the headlines. There may be a ceasefire between Croats and Muslims. But this is the reality. At Bugojno, in Central Bosnia, in October 1994, the townspeople are in the firing line. Each day there are casualties and more families lose their homes.

Bugojno is a Muslim town in the sights of Bosnian Serb forces who have artillery on hilltops less than six kilometres away. For a fortnight the Muslim forces have been trying to regain the small town of Gornji Vakuf, from which they were driven earlier in the war, and the vital road link between Bugojno and Travnik. Currently the only way to Travnik is over a dirt road.

Bugojno fathers and sons are in this battle; they take their turn on the front line. They fear for their families as shells rain down on their homes.

The Feed the Children team are equally at risk — they load aid supplies onto distribution trucks in clear view of the Serb artillerymen. Our team work in heavy bullet-proof jackets and helmets. They avoid unnecessary risks and there are times when deliveries have to be postponed because shelling is in progress or the distribution point is close to the fighting, but they do their best to keep to their delivery schedule.

Monthly deliveries are made to numerous distribution centres in towns and rural areas. At each there is a list of the displaced families and 'social cases' who are registered to receive aid there. They sign for what they are given.

What they receive depends on the size of their family; the age of their children. Our team have produced statistics for each location. They know how many babies there are, how many toddlers, school-children, pregnant and lactating women, elderly in need.

Many of the distribution centres are former shops, long since denuded of stock. I accompanied team members to a former village bakery. A few sacks of flour were all that remained to be shared among the 400 residents. Soon the shelves were filled with packets of cereals, tins of Heinz baby meals, Nutricia baby cereal, boxes of pasta, tins of meat, bars of soap, bottles of disinfectant from the Feed the Children truck. Then came the bulk items, sacks of rice and bags of full-cream milk powder. Together with the vegetables from the surrounding fields, this food would keep the villagers going for another month.

Back to the warehouse; load up, and set out again.

We dodge around shell craters and rubble from a recent artillery attack. We pass houses destroyed by shell-fire or burnt out during 'ethnic cleansing'. Whole communities have been destroyed; there are rows of houses gutted and without windows and roofs. Here and there are small communities that appear untouched by the war; then there is a single gutted house, where a Croat family had lived.

Our destination this time is a remote mountain village. The last six miles are along a rocky track, through farmyards and across streets. We need to use four-wheel drive even though the weather is good and the ground hard and dry. We stop in a clearing outside the local store and are immediately surrounded by dozens of children, hoping that — just like a month ago — we have bars of chocolate for them. They are not disappointed.

After delivering the aid to a village elder in charge of distribution we are invited into a house for coffee. Apples and walnuts are offered and accepted. We note for next month that the children need clothing and shoes.

The deliveries continue day after day. With winter approaching, the villagers' own produce will soon be gone. There is no employment; they have no money to buy the commercial supplies that are reaching the shops in Bugojno. We must return.

A BIHAC TRAGEDY

by MALCOLM TURNER
CAZIN, NORTH-WEST BOSNIA, 12 FEBRUARY 1995

Mirella Mustedangic is my interpreter. She has been working for me just a few short weeks. She is an attractive young woman, married with lovely 2-year-old twin daughters, Una and Nera. She has a nice house and a handsome husband, and if she were an

English girl then at the age of 24 she would stand confidently on the threshold of life with the rosiest of futures.

But today Mirella is desperately unhappy.

She is unhappy because she cannot live in her nice house. Her children have known nothing but war. She lives in constant fear of bombardment. She cannot travel much beyond the town in which she now dwells. She cannot give her children nice things and, worst of all, she now has to regard her handsome husband as one of the enemy. Because this is not England, it is north-west Bosnia.

Mirella has always lived in north-west Bosnia, in the town of Velika Kladusa. And it was here that she met and married her husband, Edin. Life was good then. Family holidays with uncles, aunts and cousins, joining the annual trek to Porec on Istra, a peninsula on the Adriatic coast. Employment was never a problem, and there was plenty of money and time to enjoy the beautiful countryside. There was no significance in a person's name and there was no thought of war.

But in 1991, when Slovenia declared independence, and Croatia immediately followed suit, it all changed. Serbia declared war on Croatia and, in the year following, interfactional fighting broke out in Bosnia. Suddenly it became important if your name was Vlado, or Jusuf, or Slobodan, because it identified you as Croat, Muslim or Serb.

Mirella and her husband are Muslims. Not in the ordinary way of things. They ate pork, they drank slivovic, and they rarely, if ever, attended the mosque. Mirella is a modern woman with Western tastes and has never worn a veil. They never fasted during Ramadan. Nonetheless they are Muslims.

The war between Serbia and Croatia came to an unresolved halt; but the fighting continued in Bosnia with the Bosnian Serbs claiming large tracts of land to the east and west of the country, gripping the central territories held by Croats and Muslims like a claw.

Within the Bosnian Serb controlled territories, Muslim 'pockets' were created. Islands of Muslims in a sea of Serbs.

Mirella and her husband were caught in one of these pockets, the Bihac Pocket, right in the north-west extremity of the country. Strictly speaking, it shouldn't be a pocket because it shares a common, internationally recognized border with Croatia; but a pocket it is, as that part of Croatia is held by the Serbs in what is known as the Republic of Serbian Krajina.

Bad enough, but here there is a particularly hideous twist. The pocket, which is approximately the size of the Isle of Wight, is itself divided. To the south; the 5th Corp of the BiH Armija and to the north, in a small enclave, the army of West Bosnia led by the business-man, Fikret Abdic. This enclave is centred on Velika Kladusa and it is where the bitterest fighting is taking place. Muslim versus Muslim, kith versus kin.

And it was where Mirella and her husband lived.

There was little choice for a man in a society where brutality was commonplace and the rule of the mob holds sway. And so Mirella's husband had no option but to fight for 'Fikret's Army'. Then one day after a 5th Corp incursion he was captured and taken to Coralici where he was held and beaten, suffering severe bruising and two broken ribs. A period of incarceration followed and one can only guess at what coercive methods were used. He was eventually released to fight again, this time for the 5th Corp. So, by design or by insensitivity, we shall never know, he was sent to the front line in the north to fight his erstwhile comrades-in-arms.

During the time of his imprisonment, Mirella came to a momentous decision. Velika Kladusa was in danger of being overrun by the more numerous troops of 5th Corp. There was fighting in the streets. Her husband was in the southern pocket and she had family in Cazin. She decided to make a break across the frontline under the cover of night, carrying her two small children. Luck was with her through the fear-filled night, and she was able to walk the twenty-five kilometres or so without being challenged. She was reunited with an uncle and his family who offered her a place to stay. She joined sixteen other family members and refugees under the one roof.

That was three months ago.

At the time Mirella made her escape from Velika Kladusa she had no way of knowing of the whereabouts of Edin. Later she learned of his release from prison and deployment to the frontline eleven days before her escape. She was never to be reunited with him.

Mirella's belief that 5th Corp would take Velika Kladusa proved prescient and the town fell, creating twenty-four thousand refugees who were housed in the chicken shacks and razed houses in the camps of Batnoga and Tiranj. But 'Fikret's Army' was regrouping and, on 18 December 1994, in a counter-offensive, the town was regained with the confrontation line forced back to its original position.

During the exchanges Mirella's husband was once again taken prisoner. This time by his former confederates.

At the time of writing it is not known what happened to him while he was detained. One can only conjecture. But what is known is that he has been released and has been pressed into frontline service yet again!

Mirella does not know how to deal with this news. While he was in prison, detained by the West Bosnians, she feared for his safety, knowing that he might suffer afresh the beatings and abuse. But now he is again a soldier with his weapons pointing at the town where his wife and children live. Edin has a brother who is in the 5th Corp in the north-east of the pocket near Busim and even as I write it is entirely possible that the brothers face each other across the confrontation line.

Mirella has heard through a friend who works for Feed the Children in Velika Kladusa, that he is severely depressed and the separation from his wife and daughters has led to thoughts of suicide. The same friend has passed a message saying he wishes Mirella to return to Velika Kladusa so they can be together.

But Mirella cannot go to Velika Kladusa, she does not know what fate would await her there. She would once again have to put her life, and those of her children, at great risk to cross the confrontation line. And if she got there she could find that the town had once again been taken by the 5th Corp. Or that Edin had been taken prisoner for the third time. Or that he had fallen casualty to the war and she had been left friendless in a hostile town.

And so she stays put.

Mirella works for me now, and as we drive around the pocket on Feed the Children business I am conscious of those quiet moments when I know she is undergoing a tumult of emotion. As she sits silently alongside me in the car, I feel a sense of utter powerlessness to help. I rail at the forces that inflict such problems on a young woman. Problems that will not be solved even at the ending of the war.

There are lighter moments when we are able to laugh and tease. Then I look at her and think how it would be if she were a young woman in England. I have never heard her say she would like to be English, so I suspect she has a pride in being Bosnian and a Muslim. But I'd bet my next year's beer money she would exchange her problems for an English girl's any day!

OUT OF THE
FIRING LINE
BUT STILL IN THE
FIRE

by PETER ANNEREAU
PROCUREMENT MANAGER, FEED THE CHILDREN, 24 JULY 1995

The fall of Srebrenica, one of the so-called UN safe areas in Eastern Bosnia, to Bosnian Serb forces on 11 July 1995, led to one of the biggest forced movements of people since fighting started in former Yugoslavia in 1992. This is the story of the people of a town besieged for three years, whom the outside world were unable to feed or protect.

The people of Srebrenica had endured more of the misery of the war in Bosnia than most of the country's four million population long before their enclave was overrun by the surrounding Serb forces on 11 July 1995.

The town, swelled to 50,000 by refugees from the surrounding district, had been under siege for three years with only sporadic food supplies getting in from the outside world for many months.

The world was threatening to intervene on their behalf, but had only provided a small peace-keeping force of Dutch soldiers who, despite a late air strike by NATO planes, were unable to prevent the Serbs overpowering the lightly-armed defenders.

When the end came, the worst fears of the townsfolk were realized. All males deemed to be of an age to fight were rounded up. Some were said to have been killed, girls raped and taken away to an unknown fate along with the men. Women, children and the elderly were put on buses and driven to the front line between Serb and Bosnian Government-held territories.

Distraught and weary, they eventually reached

'safety' on foot and were taken to the airfield at Tuzla, where a 'tent city' had been hastily set up.

Many were soon sent on to collective centres in towns throughout the Tuzla district where space was provided in schools and other public buildings.

At Tuzla airfield, more and more arrived, registrations eventually topping 27,000, almost all of whom were women and children.

Alenka Tanovic, a Tuzla girl working with the UN to register the refugees on arrival, told me they had horrific stories of atrocities and were beside themselves with grief at being separated from husbands and sons, whom they feared they would never see again.

She said: 'During the twelve hours I worked there — from 9pm to nine the next morning — between 9,000 and 10,000 people were registered. During all that time I did not see a single male over the age of 13, or a man under 60. The stories they told were horrific and will haunt me for ever.'

The refugees had only a bag or two of possessions each, some only the clothes they stood up in, and told of bags and money being taken off them as they were put on buses by the Bosnian Serb soldiers.

One woman to whom I spoke held an outstretched hand towards me: 'I have lost my husband and four sons,' she said, indicating their fate by drawing a finger across her throat.

My own arrival at the camp coincided with a rumour that thousands of Srebrenica men had escaped capture and had found their way on foot through forests to reach safety.

Hundreds of women — many clutching babies and children — moved en masse to the registration area as a truck arrived. They strained to see if they could recognize any of the men. But the rumour appeared exaggerated, and the camp intake was swollen by only 150 that day.

As UN troops from Scandinavia tried to hold them back, women groaned and wailed, burying their faces in their hands and collapsing to the ground. There were a few joyous and tearful reunions, but for most there was no news.

Earlier, one woman had hanged herself.

When Mrs Sadiku Ogata, the UN High Commissioner for Refugees, arrived by helicopter to see conditions in the camp, a number of women remonstrated with her over what they felt had been an inadequate response to their plight by the UN.

Mrs Ogata spent about an hour in the camp, speaking to families and looking at the medical facilities before holding talks with local government officials and UN agency staff in Tuzla.

The camp itself was well organized and, when I was there, housed around 6,000 people in low, circular tents, many of which were overcrowded with ten or more adults and children.

The tents were set out in blocks of forty-eight on the grassy ground either side of the concrete runway, which reflected the heat of the mid-summer sun from which there was little shelter. I saw one boy of about 7 with arms and shoulders heavily creamed to combat painful sunburn.

A number of children with high temperatures and coughs were being comforted by mothers and grandmothers in sad-faced groups lying around in their tents and under improvised awnings.

Though the weather was hot and sunny, there were areas where water was lying on the hard-packed clay following a short storm. It was clear that if the weather turned wet conditions would rapidly deteriorate.

Realizing the unsuitability of the camp for long-term use, local authorities set up collective centres initially in seven towns, but later increased this. Most were housed in schools, but as this would cause local children to miss their lessons when the new term began, once again this was only a temporary solution to the Muslims' growing refugee housing crisis. Elsewhere some refugees have been living in such centres for up to three years.

I visited a sports hall at Banovici, some twenty-five miles away. One of seven new refugee centres in a town that already had thousands of displaced people from earlier in the war, the building was overflowing with women with babes in arms, children at hand, and elderly relatives.

They were lying on blankets spread out over the sports hall floor, most without mattresses and all without any privacy or separation from the next sad group. There were even families lying and sitting in the indoor soccer goals at either end of the hall. They were lying in the hallway and side rooms, they were drawing water from a tap beside the road 50 metres away, and there were lines of wet washing on fences and strings.

But the unsuitability of the premises was appreciated by the Banovici authorities, and when I returned next day the main hall had been cleared by billeting people on local households. An official explained that the town had been shelled and there were fears that there would be many casualties if the glass-sided sports centre was hit.

Of Banovici's 3,000 new refugees, over 40 per cent were children.

By Saturday 23 July — with the fall of Zepa, a second UN 'safe area' appearing to be imminent — further arrangements were being made to house Srebrenica refugees in additional locations. How desperate the overall refugee crisis was became evident as it was announced that more than 500 were to be taken to Brka, which had been evacuated in the past and is only 3½ km from the front line at the most northerly point of Bosnia, where Serbs control a narrow corridor of land crucially important to them for getting supplies to all Serb-held territories in Western Bosnia.

To people newly escaped from Srebrenica, the

prospect of being moved to another front line was a further cruel blow.

Meanwhile, on the evening of Wednesday 19 July, reports in Tuzla that Zepa, the second eastern enclave had fallen, brought a flurry of activity as aid agencies got together to polish up plans to help the inevitable influx of refugees, who were expected to cross into government-held territory near Kladanj, 40 km south of Tuzla for resettlement in towns around Zenica. These towns already have many displaced people and many more residents needing support from aid agencies.

Nowhere in northern Bosnia is far from a front line. Tuzla, the capital of a district of more than a million people, is only approachable via tortuous tracks through forests. All supplies have to go along them, the drivers of large trucks and coaches having to call on all their experience to negotiate the bumpy, twisty, steep and sometimes muddy-rutted tracks. On sections close to lines of confrontation, where shelling and sniping are common, UN armoured corps provide escort. A journey with supplies from the Croatian coast frequently takes twelve hours.

Many areas are subject to sporadic shelling. One person was killed and nine injured in Tuzla last week as a result of a single Serb shell.

With fighting continuing at Zepa (as of Sunday 23 July), a large-scale attack on the Bihac Pocket — yet another UN declared 'safe area' in the north-west of Bosnia — plus threats from world leaders of 'decisive' action in response to further Serb assaults, indications were that a turning point in the war was close at hand.

REPORT FROM TUZLA

by MICHELLE ROBBINS
26 JULY 1995

The air of expectancy as we all waited was almost tangible. Finally at 9pm the first people appeared out of the darkness. They were women, children and old men. All looked utterly exhausted and they were mostly silent. Many of the women carried babies; everyone carried bundles of belongings tied up with string. The PAKBAT soldiers and UNHCR staff were brilliant. They shepherded people up the bank to collect their ration packs, coffee and blankets. Some supported those who were clearly on the point of collapse and carried their belongings. We approached women with babies to guide them to our tent. Some of the bundles I carried were almost too heavy to lift, yet these women had carried them 7-8 kilometres as well as carrying babies and trying to keep hold of other children. Their clothes were saturated with sweat from the exertion. Some of the people had left their villages early the day before and walked to Zepa where they spent the night sleeping on the ground. At 2pm they had been loaded on to buses and brought to the edge of no man's land. They were a tragic sight.

The fact that we were able to offer help was announced over the loud hailer system and in no time at all the tent was full of women and babies. Many of the women put their babies down on the blankets and flopped down beside them. Their fingers were so stiff from carrying their bundles they were totally unable to begin removing the babies' clothing and washing them. The babies were all wrapped in layers of clothing, all of it old and much of it knitted. Laura, Rosimira and I looked after dozens of babies during the next three hours. None of them had any nappies and all of them were in urine soaked clothing. Our biggest difficulty was that we had no clean clothing to put on the babies once we'd sorted out their nappies and plastic pants. Many of the babies had extremely bad nappy rash, requiring more than the zinc and castor oil cream we could provide, and we pointed them in the direction of the MSF tent. Lots of them were sneezing, and although our tent was warm because of the crush of bodies, I worried about them sleeping in the open shelters.

There was one very unusual family. A man of about 30, his wife and child. He was tall, fit and well dressed. He was also clearly well educated. His wife was traumatized and he attended to both his baby and his wife. I was amazed by his outward calmness. How he had managed to escape was a mystery. He was now managing to behave totally naturally with his baby, talking and laughing with her as he put on her nappy. He was also self possessed enough to return later for spare nappies. It would have been fascinating to talk with him, but his first priority had to be settling his family, and in any case we were far too busy to stop and talk.

Some time after midnight buses began ferrying people on the next stage of their journey and we decided to try and get some sleep. I settled down with a blanket close to Steve and Laura who fell asleep almost immediately. Half an hour or so later I heard people moving around the tent and discovered a nurse from MSF with a mother and baby. They were looking for nappies. By the light of my torch I looked after the last baby of the night with the sound of gunfire in the background. Back under my blanket I shivered my way through the night. It was bitterly cold and I hoped the refugees would be able to keep each other warm simply because there were so many people in a small space. Throughout the night messages continued over the loud hailer and by morning I guessed half of the arrivals of the night before had been moved.

Thursday 27th July. We got up before 6am to hear that a second wave of refugees were due in. It was still quite cold and there was a heavy morning mist. My hair was soaking wet within minutes. The first people began arriving at 6.30am and by 8am it was bedlam in our tent.

I looked after one baby boy whose mother had bound his legs together. I suppose it made it easier for her to carry him. The look of delight when I removed the binding was unforgettable. He had no nappy and, like all the others, he was soaking wet. Another little baby who just would not stop crying was put into a blanket by his mother. Then she and her daughter swung it to and fro as you could a hammock. It looked very rough to me so I peeped in to see how he was faring. He was totally unperturbed, rolling around happily in the bottom of the blanket.

Despite the hustle and bustle I found it very easy to talk to all the babies I looked after, telling both them and their mothers what beautiful babies they were and that they were safe now. I know they didn't understand a word I was saying, but from the smiles and gurgles I knew I was getting my message across. It felt very important to let these women and children, who had been through so much, know that there were people who cared what happened to them. And it was easy because the babies really were gorgeous. Some were blond and blue eyed, others dark with deep brown eyes. How anyone could tell whether they were Muslim or Croat, or anything else for that matter, was beyond my comprehension, and why on earth should it matter anyway? Almost all of the babies responded with gummy smiles and gurgles and at one point, while gently wiping a bonny baby girl with baby-wipes, a rocket was fired in the distance. The contrast was obscene and I felt desperately sad for these people who had lost so much.

Our big problem this morning was shortage of plastic pants, a lack of clean baby clothes and no bags for mothers to take away the soiled clothing. Because the babies had no nappies, many came with clothes that were so soiled they all had to be totally removed. I ended up wrapping babies in nappies and using the cellophane the nappies came in to wrap the soiled clothes. The mothers couldn't simply throw them away because they had nothing else.

One mother and her daughter made a particular impact on me today. Amela and her beautiful daughter Asla. Amela spoke a little English and had a lovely serene face. She had been forced to leave her husband, her father and her uncle behind in Zepa. Her eyes filled with tears when she spoke of them. She was obviously very happy when I enthused over Asla and when we had finished said, 'Thank you very much', again and again. This moved me more than I can say. I was giving her just basic essentials and she was so grateful. They came back several times in the twenty-four hours they were in the camp. Finally Amela brought Asla to say goodbye. I wrote down their names and she asked for mine. They were bound for Zenica and I said that I would try to contact them there. I wanted to give Asla one of the toys I'd brought with me from England which I'd left at the house in Tuzla.

Later in the day another little girl, Leila, really enjoyed having a bath in one of the baby boxes. I wondered how long it would be before she'd be able to have another.

As the day was less frantic than yesterday we were able to take more notice of the condition of the people. They were obviously poor and lived quite simple lives. Their clothes were old and tattered, their teeth were mainly broken and decaying. Many of the babies had rashes and often had horrendously scaly black scalps from lack of washing. I took one baby girl to the MSF tent, her scalp was so bad. The medics just said, 'Shampoo'.

One little baby was brought to the MSF tent by its mother with the remains of its umbilical cord black on its stomach. The medics treated it with antiseptic, put on a dressing and sent mother and baby on their way. Another, brought into our tent for a nappy change, had a very sunburnt face. The MSF doctor was with us at the time but offered no treatment, so I gently rubbed on some baby lotion. I let her lie on the blanket with no clothes on for fifteen minutes or so by which time she looked a lot cooler. The problem was that the women were so disorientated they were wandering around with their babies in the hot sunshine without thinking to protect them. We made sure we advised the women we spoke to about the dangers, but as the alternative was sitting in a huddle in the shelters I'm not sure how much notice they took.

By early afternoon there were over 1,000 refugees in the camp, and the latrines were becoming a health hazard. The first coaches did not leave for Zenica until 8.15pm. How they would fare on the long journey was not something I wanted to dwell on. Further refugees were expected 'at any time', so it was necessary to make room for them. Also UNHCR and the local authorities were keen to complete the move to more permanent accommodation as quickly as possible. In the event no more refugees arrived that evening and so we all had time to clean the camp ready for the next arrivals.

Before retiring we had a chat with one of the MSF medics. He told us that one of their people had gone out along the route to collect dead bodies. He'd filled his car then came across four wounded Muslim soldiers. For reasons best known to him he hid them, planning to return later to pick them up. When he did return the Serbs had got there first and all four were dead.

By 9.30pm we were tucked up in our sleeping bags and I slept soundly, falling asleep with the sound of the gunfire that had continued all day, in the background. My knees were really sore from crawling around on the rough blankets after nappies, pins, etc., and my leg muscles ached from getting up and down. I hadn't realized it but I was obviously getting more exercise than when I play squash. However, I made a mental note to recommend that changing tables should be used in the future.

Friday 28th July. Despite the news that more refugees were expected at any time from 11am yesterday, we slept through the night and were woken by Esther (UNHCR) who told us they were due in forty-five minutes. We struggled out of our bags and into the morning mist. Then luxury, a cup of coffee made by PAKBAT. Everyone stood around in clusters awaiting the new arrivals. Over the CODAN we heard that Nick had got out of the Krajina but the Serbs had confiscated his computer. Finally at 8.15am the next wave of people from Zepa began to trickle into the camp. God knows what they'd felt in the hours they'd been kept hanging about before being herded onto the buses. Many were quicker at settling down than the previous group. They were mainly middle aged or very elderly. There weren't so many babies as in the two previous groups. However, we did have a bit of a rush and then got involved with MSF staff who were desperate for a bottle to give water to a baby that was just a few days old. It was too weak to take milk from its mother. It had had a spasm and there was the possibility that it had a chest infection. Mother and baby stayed almost two hours in the MSF tent during which time one of their staff went off to their warehouse to try to find a bottle. Before he returned both the woman and her baby went off into the crowd. They were soon to be packed onto a bus and sent off to Zenica. I couldn't believe what I was seeing. From what I had seen and heard I had grave doubts that the baby would survive the journey. I thought for no more than a minute before dashing across to Marguerite in the UNHCR tent and describing the situation. She was brilliant and asked me to take her to the woman. I practically ran all the way, followed by Marguerite and her interpreter. He decided to give me a hard time saying, 'It is normal for babies to have spasms; it is not normal for them to be hot. Babies often get problems with their umbilical cords', and finally, 'Are you a doctor?' I stood my ground and was supported by Marguerite who agreed with me that the baby was in no state to travel. At that point Marguerite arranged to take mother and baby to the clinic in Kladanj and arranged for the rest of the family to leave on the last coach which would stop by the clinic and pick them up. When Marguerite returned she said that the baby had been given some fluid and the mother had been given more for the journey. She had also been given a long list of the various aspects of the baby's condition that needed to be checked out for the medical people in Zenica. Clearly the little one was not out of the woods yet.

Throughout the morning and into the afternoon buses continued to leave for the Zenica area. One little group that was there till the end was a woman with a baby and three older children. We'd looked after the baby and the woman had seen the MSF staff. She'd returned with a heavily bandaged foot. The older children were very scruffy and the best I could do was to clean their faces with babywipes. The little girl, Fatima, was absolutely delighted; the little boys pulled faces! Gordon tried to find out their story but was hampered by not having an interpreter around. However, we did discover that the baby was the child of the woman and the other three children belonged to a man who had been held in Zepa. Their mother had apparently left them several years previously. I wonder if she'll come looking for them now.

As the camp emptied, a local woman and her daughter paid us a visit. They brought with them the most delicious plateful of a local delicacy consisting of filo pastry and cheese, plus a dish of yoghurt. Gordon, Diane and I sat on the blankets in the tent and scoffed the lot. Gordon managed to convey his appreciation in Bosnian. Diane and I had to make do with much rolling of eyes and smiles.

Since the camp was now empty of refugees Gordon

decided to go back to Tuzla for the night. He gave me a lift back to have a shower and change my clothes. While in Tuzla there was the sound of automatic gun-fire that was obviously within the city limits. Much refreshed I returned with John to wait with Diane and Gary for new arrivals.

Later as we lay down to sleep we heard some Muslim soldiers arguing with a PAKBAT soldier. We weren't sure what was going on but understood them to be talking about our baby food that was stacked up outside. One of the soldiers — it might have been the one that gave Diane and me a hard time the night before — took his gun off his shoulder and was very aggressive to the PAKBAT soldier. Di and I looked out through the tent windows making it very obvious we were watching the proceedings. Eventually the three Muslims walked away and the PAKBAT soldier went off in another direction. As we settled back down again a man with a gun over his shoulder walked past the tent flap. The silhouette was menacing and I was again reminded that the situation here was far from 'normal'.

To my dismay I then developed a case of Bosnia Belly and spent an extremely miserable night trooping to and from the latrines.

DEFINITIONS

These definitions are extracted from the following sources:
Article 19 glossary, 'Forging War'.
Ed Vulliamy, 'Seasons in Hell'.
Mark Almond, 'Europe's Backyard War'.
Morton, 'Serbo-Croat dictionary'.

ČETNIK — Before the formation of the Yugoslav State in 1918, *četniks* (*četnici*) were irregular units within the Serbian army. In royal Yugoslavia (1918-41) the name was linked with Serb nationalist paramilitarism. In the Second World War, the term came to mean the guerrilla forces of Serbs and Montenegrins, including officers and men of the former royal Yugoslav army, which wanted to restore the kingdom of Yugoslavia with Serbian dynasty. These forces committed many atrocities against Bosnian Muslims; some of them collaborated with German and Italian commanders against the Partisan forces led by Josip Broz-Tito. Taboo in Tito's Yugoslavia, in 1990 the name was rehabilitated by extreme nationalist groups in Serbia, paving the way for armed irregular bands of volunteers to be raised and armed to fight in Croatia (and later in Bosnia). Vojislav Seselj of the SRS is the best-known leader (*vojvoda*) of the latter-day *četnici*. In Croatia, by 1991, the name had become an all-purpose description of any Serb irregular, with or without *četnik* insignia. Croat nationalists are liable to apply the term to any Serb who does not denounce Serb nationalism.

JNA — Jugoslovenska Narodna Armija, Yugoslav People's Army. As the successor to Tito's Partisan movement, the JNA was an institutional and ideological pillar of Yugoslavia. The JNA ceased to exist in May 1992, when the VJ was formed as the army of the 'new' Yugoslavia, the SRJ.

VJ — Vojska Jugoslavie, Army of Yugoslavia.

SRJ — Savezna Republika Jugoslavija.

HOS — Hrvatske Oruzare Snage, Croatian Armed Forces. A militia mustered and deployed by the extreme nationalist HSP (Hrvatska Stranka Prava, Croatian Party of Right) in Croatia in 1991 and in Bosnia in 1992.

GRANATA — This term is used by people to describe any

shell or mortar. It generally covers mines and grenades as well.

IMAM — This is the Islamic religious figure who is the leader of the mosque. They have a powerful role in Islamic societies both as religious and secular leaders.

TEKIJA — This is a Turkish word that is very rarely used. It is a large plate or dish used by Muslims. It is also used to describe a Muslim quarter of town when it is flat. Normally this Muslim quarter is called a '*mahalla*'.

SOKAK — This is a Turkish word for a street.

HVO — The Bosnian Croat Army.

HALAL — This is an Islamic term for the preparation and giving of meat without payment. During Byram (Muslim equivalent of Christmas) lamb or other meat is cut up and given 'from the heart' to relatives and neighbours. The butchering is prefaced with considerable ceremony.

BiH — Bosnia-Hercogovina.

JUKA — Nickname of unsavoury leader (including his group).

RAKIA — Local Brandy-type drink.

KAJANA — Small knife.

USTASA — Extremist group.

ARMIJA — Army.

SPANBAT — Spanish Battalion.

BRITFOR — British Forces.

UNHCR — United Nations High Commission for Refugees.

UNPROFOR — United Nations Protection Force.

PAKBAT — Pakistani Battalion.

MSF — Médecins sans Frontieres.

CODAN — High frequency communication equipment.

NGO — Non-Government Organization.

PEOPLE
TO
PEOPLE

CHILDREN FROM BRITAIN

From one Mother to another -
if only your life was as
secure as ours are here in
England. You are in my
thoughts.

...nace however you wish - for a photo of your family, a message or a
...ng. We will place it in your baby-box before delivery.

This box for your child is a gift from a friend.

This is our new baby
grandaughter - Jasmine
With our love to another
little, less fortunate,
baby.

children's drawing. ...ou wish - for a photo of your family, a message or a
We will place it in your baby-box before delivery.

One box
from
each
of
us

We wish you peace in your country and send our
love.

It is impossible for us to imagine what you
are going through, but we hope this small box
may help to make your life a little less difficult.
We pray for you and your people every day.
God bless you. Love from
Marie-Christine Medin
Christopher

Do use this space however you wish - for a photo of your family, a message or a
children's drawing. We will place it in your baby-box before delivery.

Our little great-grandson Callum, sends his love and greetings to your baby

May peace soon come to your lovely land.

This is a girl and it is me.

Love

This is made by me.

Laura christina Markham Age SIX Sir!.

I hope your baby brings you as much happiness as my little niece Elizabeth brings to my Family

We send this with and love and would ask you to pass on our love to your neighbours whatever their race or bread.

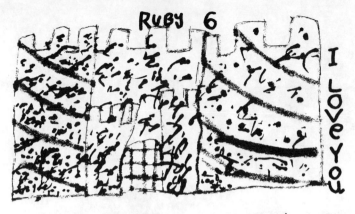

RUBY 6
I LOVE YOU

mum
dad
me

Dear people hope you find
a new home
sue and John xxxxxxxxxx love from clair

In the past I have had happy holidays
in your beautiful country with my own
children, all now grown up. We found
happiness and friendship then and I
should like to give you this small gift
in the hope that it will be useful and
that the awful troubles will soon be
over.

With love from

I SEND YOU LOVE AND HOPE FOR A SAFE

AND HAPPY FUTURE. YOU ARE NOT

FORGOTTON BUT REMAIN IN THE THOUGHTS

AND HEARTS OF MYSELF AND MANY OTHERS.

KEEP SAFE.

LINDA ASHTON

Rachael Lucy Ian Samantha Helen.C Me (Helen)

We All helped raise the Mony for your box

Do use this space however you wish - for a photo of your family, a message or a children's drawing. We will place it in your baby-box before delivery.

Birthday. The best gift I could ever dream of having is to be abel to save you childs Life.

Love KATE xxx
xx
x

Ova kutija za vaše dijete je poklon od prijatelja.

This box for your child is a gift from a friend.

love from Gowen

Do use this space however you wish - for a photo of your family, a message or a children's drawing. We will place it in your baby-box before delivery.

LETTERS OF THANKS

Thank you so much for the packages, which make me very happy. For the past three years, I have not been able to eat many of the things that you have sent.
My name is
Nermin Piralic

Ciao!
My name is Vukovic Dijana. I am 16 years old and I'm in the first level of Secondary School for nurses in Bihac. I really am so happy that I can send you a letter. I want also to thank you for the gifts that you sent to us. I hope that we can keep in touch, and that maybe one day when this war is finished that we will be able to see each other.
In this war my dad has died. Now I am living alone with my mother, and two sisters. I am sending you my picture to introduce myself. With warm regards from Bihac.

i
Cao,
Ja se zovem Vukovic' Dijana.
Imam 16. godina idem u Ira
Med'icinske skole.
Veoma mi je dvago sto se
dopisivati s vama,
Zelim da vam se zahvalim
darovima.
Nadam se da ce mose ube
muci dopisivati i kad presta
i mozda i vidjeti
liter moga.

Ciao -
My name is Sanja
Kecalovic. I am twelve
years old, and I am in the
sixth level of primary
school. Thank you very
much for all the packages
that you gave us, I am so
happy when I see that
someone cares about the
children in this war.
Goodbye -

Ćao!
Zovem se Sanja Kecalović, imam 12
godina i idem u VI razred. Puno vam
se zahvaljujem na ovim paketicima
koje ste poklonili mama djeci, neoma
sam radosna jer vidim da ima neko
ko se brine za nas djecu u ovom
prokletom ratu. Eto toliko za soda.

BAJ !

AGA PRIJATELICE

se zovem Vuković Azra.
a 12 godina. Želim da vam
hvalim na onim paketima
nam, vi se bu nas mnogo
ete, Eto nemam više ništa
kažem. Još nešto da ti
ĆAO HAJ
BAJ
Azra
HSKA bb
HAĆ

My dear friends:
I am Azra Vukovic, and I am twelve
years old. I wish to say thank you for all
of these packages. I know that you are
taking care of us. I want to say only one
thing - Ciao — and hi — bye!
I hope that we are able to keep in touch.

Ciao -
Hello buddies, my friends,
This opportunity to send you a letter, in these hard days, gives me a great deal of pleasure. I am living in this crazy war, and have lost a lot of my close friends. But that is not everything I miss. I am missing love, and I want to feel that. Man can not have any special knowledge for building a friendship bridge, because of that give me your hand, and give me a few warm words in writing. As many children in my country, I have one big wish, that is to stop this war as soon as possible. I hope that you share this wish. Because it is really painful when you realize how many children of your age have been killed, or arrested, and are now prisoners. My message is: Don't let even one person, or one child on this planet ever know the one short word 'war', or its effect. Thank you for all the gifts that you sent and thank you for everything that you are doing for our country. Danijela Muslic, 14 years.

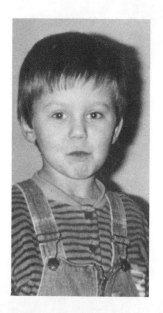

I want to say thank you to your humanitarian organization which makes us so happy. All the children from my city, Bihac, are looking forward to being able to once again get school materials and candies. I am eight years old, I have one brother who is three years old, we are sending you our regards.
Elvis and Irfam Piralic

DEAR FRIENDS IN ENGLAND!

We are pupils from Busovača, the small town in Central Bosnia. We are in the fourth grade now. Our teacher is Mrs Lucija Velte. Going to school is very dangerous here, but we are still going and try to learn as well as possible. Our friends from the humanitarian organization Feed the Children told us your address and promised that they would deliver this letter to you. By this letter, we want to thank all the children and good people in England and UK, who are sending food, clothes and everything else that we need. Thanks to good people from Feed the Children we are getting all these things. With your parcels we are receiving many letters. Some of you maybe, wrote to us, too. We are not able to answer to each of you. By this letter we want to say that we are very grateful to you for everything you do, for our care and love which you express in your letters. We appreciate it very much and hope that one day we shall be able to pay you back in some way. The best way would be if you would be our guests as soon as the peace comes back here. We could get to know each other better and become friends. We want you to find the way to inform all the people in your town about our letter and give them our best regards. We hope you will answer our letter.

Our address is: Učiteljica Lucija Velte, Osnovna Skola Busovača, Bosnia i Hercegovina.

With best wishes!

Brigita Lovrić
Josip Marković

Tihomir
Jarić

Marijeta Ljubas
Karolina Akapović
Ilija Ljubičić

Iskić Zlatko

Daniel Arapović

Robert Vuleta

Lucija Nette

Ibtana Korsćević
Katarina Colić
Goran Amdrijašević
ćosić Jelena
Bernard Brnada
Marko Vuleta
Marina Filipović
Ivan Filipović
Miroslav Cokić

Dragan Visković

Ilijana Livančić
Helena Skapić
Nataša Božić

BUILDING
THE
PEACE

NOVEMBER UPDATE

by DAVID H. W. GRUBB
FTC EXECUTIVE DIRECTOR

THE ROLE OF HUMANITARIAN AID
ORGANIZATIONS IN FORMER YUGOSLAVIA

In recent history, the number of agencies involved in humanitarian aid has grown. In Bosnia the ebb and flow of conflict has disrupted supplies of food, medical and hygiene items, prevented schools from operating and generally destroyed any kind of normal life for anyone. Simple daily tasks such as walking down the street or buying bread becomes dangerous or simply impossible. It is in such situations that different types of humanitarian aid agencies operate, specializing in helping people cope with the most life-threatening situations disasters impose.

The first agencies into a conflict are emergency aid organizations. These agencies deliver the most basic necessities to sustain life: food, water, shelter, clothing and medical aid to specific categories of people. Feed the Children plans and works jointly with other similar agencies to ensure that children of all ages are cared for in the best possible way.

Once the initial crisis is over, development agencies enter the area. These agencies help to rebuild the services a country needs to run itself by, for example, refurbishing schools, making repairs to industrial areas and retraining workers.

FEED THE CHILDREN'S RAPID RESPONSE

The most acute hardship has occurred in communities which have become cut off from supplies, surrounded by hostile forces and dependent on aid supplies being brought into towns and villages by humanitarian organizations across enemy lines. Feed the Children has often been able to get food into these besieged communities where others cannot. As a relatively small organization with teams positioned strategically all over the country, we are able to respond quickly to emergency needs. We have built up trust with governments on all sides of the conflict and so can often negotiate our way through areas that other organizations cannot.

In 1993 Feed the Children was the first independent agency in ten months of fighting to be allowed through Croat lines into the tiny Muslim enclave of Stari Vitez. In December 1994 we were the first NGO to take food into the besieged town of Bihac in six months. Since then we have been delivering regular supplies of food and hygiene materials to over 140,000 children and their carers throughout Bosnia and Croatia.

CURRENT PROGRAMMES

Feed the Children are currently working in the North-West, Central and North-East of Bosnia on a variety of programmes. The basis of our support is a monthly basic ration of supplementary food items and hygiene materials which is given to children from 0 to 5 years, pregnant and lactating women and the extremely vulnerable.

Our three main areas of operation are as follows:

North-West Bosnia

1. *Vojnic Camp.* The 25,000 people in this make-shift camp are all from the Velika Kladusa area of Bihac who were forced to Croatia due to inter-Muslim fighting. The camp stretches along 5km of road in the Krajina area of Croatia — until recently occupied by Krajinian Serbs — whose homes consist of improvised tents, backs of lorries and abandoned Serb houses. Humanitarian efforts have ensured that regular distributions of food and clean water are made, but conditions are far from perfect, particularly as the future of this isolated and unwanted group of people is uncertain. Feed the Children is distributing food and hygiene products to ten centres within the camp to approximately 11,500 children and extreme-need social cases.

2. *Bihac Pocket.* Until a few months ago the Bihac area was surrounded by Serb-held territory and because of its isolated position and difficulties of access, the pocket received fewer aid convoys than any other part of Bosnia in 1994. The last few months has seen the 'liberation' of nearly all Serb-held areas surrounding the Bihac pocket but the need for humanitarian aid continues.

Feed the Children is supporting 27,500 children and their carers through a variety of social agencies and distribution points including public kitchens, orphanages and pharmacies.

Central Bosnia

Criss-crossed by Muslim and Croat community 'borders' the central Bosnia area is a politically-sensitive area in which to work. Feed the Children has two main programmes in this area:

1. *Supplementary feeding and hygiene.* Approximately 44,000 young children and vulnerable groups are receiving food and hygiene supplies on a regular basis throughout the area.

2. *Kifle Project.* Under this programme a fresh bread roll is given to over 50,000 school children every day at school. Local committees, Non-Government Organizations and bakers are involved in drawing up contracts under which the bakers are given enough flour, sugar and milk to produce the rolls and to cover the costs of baking and distribution. This programme has been an overwhelming success and is due to double in size in the near future. Not only does it supply children with a daily staple food but this in itself encourages children to return to school — something which thousands of children have been unable to do since the war began.

North-East Bosnia

The people of Srebrenica, an Eastern Bosnian Muslim enclave, were forced to leave their homes earlier this year when Bosnian Serbs took control of the area. Most of the displaced were women, children and elderly men.

From its base in Tuzla, Feed the Children is supporting 3,500 refugees in Banovic, Zivinice and Gradacac. As well as the basic high-need ration, basic hygiene products are being distributed to all new mothers. A limited social feeding programme for a further 3,000 children in the areas of Doboj, Breko and Gradacac is also in operation where over 50 per cent of the population consists of displaced people.

Baby Boxes

In Bosnia and Croatia, mothers have little or no means to protect their new-born babies from cold and infection. In answer to this need, Feed the Children has devised a simple and effective kit called 'The Baby Box'. The Baby Box contains the basic items necessary to protect and nurture a new-born child. A typical box contains: baby soap, towelling nappies, nappy liners, disinfectant, sponge, baby shampoo, baby wipes, baby lotion, powder, cotton wool, a feeding bowl and a cup, weaning spoons and other items.

In the last year Feed the Children has supplied over 11,000 Baby Boxes to mothers in Bosnia and Croatia and reaction from recipients has been overwhelming. It has proved to be an extremely effective and valuable item of aid and the demand continues.

Education Aid

One of the results of the war has been the disruption of education. Some schools have been destroyed, others occupied. Children have been unable to attend school because they lack food or shoes, or the school is unheated in sub-zero temperatures or there is not even any basic equipment, desks, chairs, books or pens. Getting children back to school is important for many reasons. School provides structure and stability for children whose lives are insecure and dangerous. It gives them a chance to work out their traumatic experiences in words and pictures among trained pro-fessionals, and it gives an education and the chance of a better future.

Feed the Children's Education Aid programmes have included refurbishing schools damaged by the war and supplying much-needed exercise books, pens and pen-cils and blackboards. We have also supplied tens of thousands of pairs of shoes and wellington boots so that children in remote villages can walk to school.

FUTURE PROGRAMMES

This winter Feed the Children will be distributing much-needed warm clothing and boots to 120,000 chil-dren aged 3-14 years in the Bihac, Tuzla and other areas where a high percentage of refugees are currently living.

·Feed the Children hope to expand the Education Aid programme to cover the whole of Bosnia. Although schools are operating in most areas there is a dearth of even the most basic equipment. This programme would run in conjunction with the current Kifle Project and the winter clothing/footwear distribution to school-age children.

Over the years Feed the Children has worked closely with the Bosnian people, responding flexibly to their needs to ensure that the aid we deliver is as effective as possible. We constantly monitor the changing situations and alter our programme accordingly. Our commitment is to the children of Bosnia whose needs remain constant, whatever the politicians and generals decide.

ENDPIECE

When 'cease-fire' becomes 'truce' and the guns are finally removed, Feed the Children will assist in building the peace.

The surest way to revive a sense of trust and hope will be to focus on the youngest children town by town, village by village. This will help the adults in adjusting their view. Feed the Children went into Croatia and Bosnia because of the children. The future lies with them. We must assist in transforming them from children in war to children of peace.

In the last decade
as a result of war,

2 million children have died,

5 million have been forced into refugee camps and

12 million have been left homeless.

FEED THE CHILDREN
exists to bring relief directly to these
children.

TURNING COMPASSION INTO
ACTION

TAKING THE AID DIRECT

FEED THE CHLDREN (Europe)
is an international child-centred humanitarian relief
organization.

WHY CHILDREN?
*Because they are innocent, they are vulnerable
and their future depends on us.*

We *must* therefore be able to respond to the needs of children
first. As a child-centred agency, Feed the Children are also
able to do this — quickly and effectively.

WHAT CAN WE DO TO HELP?
Feed the Children takes the aid *fast* and *direct* and ensures
that vital aid *does* reach those children who need it most.

WHAT SORT OF AID DO WE DELIVER?
We find out from mothers, carers and health professionals
exactly what is needed. This way we can be sure that the
food, clothes and educational equipment we deliver will be
put to the best possible use.

WHAT NEXT?
It is vital that we are able to continue our work to help children
who have become the victims of war or natural disaster. We
are committed to giving these children hope for the future —
their future — as they move from survival to revival.

*Please help us turn your compassion into action by
helping Feed the Children*

*For further information on the work of Feed the Children
please phone (01734) 584000. If you would like to make a
donation, please phone our credit card hotline on 0990
600610 or send a cheque or postal order to: Feed the
Children FREEPOST, Reading, RG1 1BR.*

FEED THE CHILDREN – taking the aid direct
82 Caversham Road, Reading, Berkshire, RG1 8AE.
Telephone (01734) 584000   Fax (01734) 462426
Company Registration No. 2408036
Registered Charity No. 803236
For readers in North America
please telephone 416 757 1220